FACILITATING ENTREPRENEURSHIP GROWTH BY LIFTING BARRIERS

A WHITE BOOK ON WOMEN-OWNED SMALL AND MEDIUM-SIZED ENTERPRISES IN VIET NAM

DECEMBER 2023

ASIAN DEVELOPMENT BANK

ADB

© 2023 Asian Development Bank
6 ADB Avenue, Mandaluyong City, 1550 Metro Manila, Philippines
Tel +63 2 8632 4444; Fax +63 2 8636 2444
www.adb.org

Some rights reserved. Published in 2023.

ISBN 978-92-9270-533-6 (print), 978-92-9270-534-3 (electronic), 978-92-9270-535-0 (ebook)
Publication Stock No. SPR230590-2
DOI: http://dx.doi.org/10.22617/SPR230590-2

The views expressed in this publication are those of the authors and do not necessarily reflect the views and policies of the Asian Development Bank (ADB) or its Board of Governors or the governments they represent.

ADB does not guarantee the accuracy of the data included in this publication and accepts no responsibility for any consequence of their use. The mention of specific companies or products of manufacturers does not imply that they are endorsed or recommended by ADB in preference to others of a similar nature that are not mentioned.

By making any designation of or reference to a particular territory or geographic area, or by using the term "country" in this publication, ADB does not intend to make any judgments as to the legal or other status of any territory or area.

Please contact pubsmarketing@adb.org if you have questions or comments with respect to content, or if you wish to obtain copyright permission for your intended use that does not fall within these terms, or for permission to use the ADB logo.

Corrigenda to ADB publications may be found at http://www.adb.org/publications/corrigenda.

Notes:
In this publication, "$" refers to United States dollars.
Currency Unit Viet Nam Dong (D). D1 = $0.000043. Exchange rates as of May 2023.
ADB recognizes "China" as the People's Republic of China, "Korea" as the Republic of Korea, and "Vietnam" as "Viet Nam"

This White Book has been prepared with the support of the Women Entrepreneurs Finance Initiative (We-Fi) under Component 2 of the Women Accelerating Vibrant Enterprises in Southeast Asia and the Pacific (WAVES) program. The program is co-implemented by the Asian Development Bank (ADB) and the Ministry of Planning and Investment (MPI). The content of this White Book does not necessarily reflect the views of MPI, We-Fi, or ADB.

Contents

Tables, Figures, and Boxes

Tables

Figures

Boxes

Foreword

While Viet Nam's expanding economy has delivered positive growth in the wake of COVID-19, women-owned micro, small, and medium-sized enterprises (WSMEs) have continued to remain disproportionately underrepresented. Of the country's 523,124 active micro, small, and medium-sized enterprises in 2020, just 20% (105,876) were women owned.

Against this backdrop, we are pleased to present *Facilitating Entrepreneurship Growth by Lifting Barriers: A White Book on Women-Owned Small and Medium-Sized Enterprises in Viet Nam*, a publication that ADB has developed in partnership with the Agency for Enterprise Development (Ministry of Planning and Investment). The White Book is an integral part of the "Women Accelerating Vibrant Enterprises in Southeast Asia and the Pacific (WAVES)" program, funded by the Women Entrepreneurs Finance Initiative.

This White Book analyzes the performance of WSMEs in Viet Nam and the barriers they face. It also reviews the current legal framework, including existing policy support, regulatory gaps, and inefficiencies affecting the performance and growth of WSMEs.

While Viet Nam's passage of the Law on Support for SMEs in 2017 defined WSMEs as a distinct class and prioritized them for government support measures, many of these enterprises still face limited access to finance, social barriers, and other challenges. Further improvements to the legal framework are needed to create greater parity.

This report draws on a large body of knowledge and international best practices in recommending a series of measures that can unleash the untapped potential of WSMEs in Viet Nam. These include (i) establishing gender-disaggregated databases, (ii) incorporating WSMEs more integrally into specific laws, including the Law on Gender Equality, (iii) possible measures with a gender lens to implement the SME Support Law, and (iv) placing greater emphasis on knowledge dissemination and awareness-raising activities, including the promotion of women's entrepreneurship and role models. While some work has already been done to address the gender gap and the specific challenges that WSMEs face, greater efforts are needed to ensure a strong enabling environment for women-owned business moving forward.

Women-owned businesses have a crucial role to play in the country's efforts to achieve inclusive and sustainable development. We hope this White Book will provide greater insights into the untapped opportunities and remaining challenges facing WSMEs and provide a foundation for further research and policymaking initiatives to foster the continued growth and development of the sector.
We encourage government agencies, local authorities, business associations, companies, development finance institutions, and other stakeholders to use this guide to help spur the expansion of the WSME sector, which can become a strong driver of growth, job creation, and prosperity.

Winfried Wicklein
Director General
Southeast Asia Department
Asian Development Bank

Tran Duy Dong
Vice Minister
Ministry of Planning and Investment

Acknowledgments

This study is part of the Women Accelerating Vibrant Enterprises in Southeast Asia and the Pacific (WAVES) program of the Asian Development Bank (ADB), supported by the Women Entrepreneurs Finance Initiative (We-Fi).

ADB commissioned Palladium, in collaboration with Mekong Economics, to conduct the research and author this report. ADB wishes to acknowledge the contribution of the team: Adam McCarty, Nguyen Thanh Ha, Pham Hoang Ngan, Nguyen Thi Xuan Mai, Tran Thi Ngoc Diep, Le Thanh Tam, and Nguyen Thi Thu Hien (Mekong Economics), Janske van Eijck and Diana Bialus (Palladium), as well as Aurica Balmus (We-Fi Secretariat), Nishikawa Naotaka (JICA), Nguyen Thanh Giang (ADB Senior Social Development Officer – Gender), Veronica Mendizabal Joffre (ADB Senior Gender and Social Development Specialist), Gisela Garzon De La Roza, Amanda A. Satterly (ADB Principal Social Development Specialist – Gender and Development), and Kelly Hatell (ADB Senior Financial Sector Specialist). Valuable insights were provided by Donald Lambert (former Unit Head, Private Sector Development, ADB Viet Nam Resident Mission) and Keiko Nowacka (ADB Senior Social Development, Gender and Development). The team from ADB Viet Nam Resident Mission, led by Chu Hong Minh (Senior Financial Sector Officer), managed this study and provided overall guidance and supervision. Special thanks go to Tom Anderson, Aparna Rao, Harry Hill, Hoang Thi Ngoc Ha, and Victor Munagala (Mekong Economics Economists) and Sara Selleri and James Sparrow (Palladium Gender and Inclusion Specialists) for their thorough review.

The authors wish to thank Trinh Thi Huong, Deputy Director General, Agency for Enterprise Development (Ministry of Planning and Investment) cum Project Director of the WAVES Component 2 in Viet Nam and Nguyen Thi Bich Thuy, Deputy Director of SME Support Division, Agency for Enterprise Development (Ministry of Planning and Investment), who provided important and timely guidance during the implementation of this study. We would like to thank the Departments of Planning and Investment of Lao Cai, Thua Thien Hue, Lam Dong, and Can Tho provinces for their support in conducting this study. The authors also gratefully acknowledge the collaboration of the General Statistics Office in providing the 2021 Economic Census data, as well as that of women entrepreneurs in contributing to the surveys.

Abbreviations

ACRA	Accounting and Corporate Regulatory Authority
AED	Agency for Enterprise Development
ASEAN	Association of Southeast Asian Nations
AWEN	ASEAN Women Entrepreneurs' Network
CIC	Credit Information Center
CIT	Corporate income tax
CUB	Club of United Businesses
DOJ	Department of Justice
DOLISA	Department of Labor, Invalids and Social Affairs
DPI	Department of Planning and Investment
GBV	gender-based violence
GDP	gross domestic product
GSO	General Statistics Office
IDF	Investment and Development Fund
ILO	International Labour Organization
IWEO	Institute of Women and for Equal Opportunities
MIWE	Mastercard Index of Women Entrepreneurs
MOIT	Ministry of Industry and Trade
MOLISA	Ministry of Labour, Invalids and Social Affairs

MOST	Ministry of Science and Technology
MPI	Ministry of Planning and Investment
OSS	one-stop-shop
PRC	People's Republic of China
SBV	State Bank of Viet Nam
SMEs	small and medium-sized enterprises
SMEDF	Small and Medium-Sized Enterprise Development Fund
TVET	technical and vocational education and training
VAT	value-added tax
VCCI	Viet Nam Chamber of Commerce and Industry
VDB	Viet Nam Development Bank
VWU	Viet Nam Women's Union
WAVES	Women Accelerating Vibrant Enterprises in Southeast Asia and the Pacific
WBL	Women, Business, and Law
WEE	women's economic empowerment
WSF	Women's Support Fund
WSMEs	women-owned micro, small, and medium-sized enterprises

Abstract

Viet Nam had 523,124 active micro, small and medium-sized enterprises (SMEs), of which 105,876 (20%) were women-owned in 2020. These women-owned micro, small, and medium-sized enterprises (WSMEs), on average, employ fewer workers and are less likely to be joint-stock companies. The rapidly expanding economy of Viet Nam has led to rapid growth across all sectors, but WSMEs continue to be disproportionately represented. This White Book—the first of its kind—provides an overview of WSMEs (characteristics, performance, and barriers) and reviews the legal framework (policy support, regulatory gaps, or inefficiencies) impacting WSMEs. The primary inquiry driving its analysis is what factors contribute to the fact that women in contemporary Viet Nam control only 20% of operational SMEs and just 11% of large enterprises. The analysis aims to examine the hindrances and regulatory gaps that WSMEs face and provide recommendations on effective measures to support them. The White Book uses the definition of SMEs specified in the SME Support Law. It draws mainly on data from the first national database on WSMEs from the 2021 Economic Census collected by the General Statistics Office (GSO) of Viet Nam, as well as additional desk research, surveys, interviews, and consultations.

While there are improvements to be made to the legal framework, there are primarily obstacles outside Viet Nam's legal framework that continue to impede the growth of WSMEs and that remain to be addressed. Specifically, most SME legal and policy documents reviewed do not adequately incorporate clear and distinct references to women, gender, and women-owned businesses, and this could partially explain why women do not feel particularly well-supported by national government policy and programming. For example, only 4 out of 11 legal documents reviewed specifically mention women in at least one instance (SME Support Law, 2017; National Strategy on Gender Equality, 2021–2030; Law on Gender Equality, 2006; and Decision No. 939/QD-TTg dated 30 June 2017 approving the program for supporting women in entrepreneurship during 2017–2025). Meanwhile, many barriers, such as the unequal distribution of household responsibilities between men and women, are rooted in underlying societal norms. Men also monopolize many business networking opportunities, creating an environment where women experience a lesser sense of comfort and acceptance compared to men.

This report concludes with recommendations on the continued establishment of gender-disaggregated databases, the incorporation of WSMEs into certain laws such as the Law on Gender Equality, a strategic rethinking about how to implement the SME Support Law with a gender lens, and a stronger emphasis on knowledge dissemination and awareness-raising activities, including the promotion of women's entrepreneurship and role models. While much work has been done to address the gender gap and the specific challenges faced by WSMEs, more needs to be done to provide an enabling environment with regard to opportunities for women doing business in Viet Nam.

1 Introduction

Micro, small, and medium-sized enterprises (SMEs[1]) play a crucial role in the economic growth of Viet Nam. They constitute over 97% of all enterprises[2] and generate 36% of total employment.[3] Of the active SMEs in Viet Nam, women own 20% (105,876), while men own 80% (417,248). A majority of the active women-owned micro, small, and medium-sized enterprises (WSMEs) are micro (69%) and small (28%). Medium-sized WSMEs represent only 3% of total WSMEs compared with 5% for men-owned SMEs. Approximately 46% of all WSMEs operate in the wholesale and retail trade and motor vehicle and motorcycle repair sectors. On average, WSMEs had fewer employees and were less likely to be joint-stock companies, although reported average revenues and profits were much the same as men-owned SMEs. Despite their significance, little research has been conducted to investigate the differences between men-owned and women-owned SMEs.

Women entrepreneurs encounter various financial and nonfinancial obstacles that deter them from realizing their full business potential. Access to finance is one of the greatest constraints faced by women entrepreneurs and their enterprises.[4] There is a financing gap because WSMEs face different challenges compared to their male counterparts, which are not addressed by financial institutions with adapted products and services. According to a survey conducted by the World Bank in 2020 across 190 countries, 90% have at least one regulation that hinders women-led SMEs' access to finance. Additionally, in 18 countries, men can legally prevent their wives from working outside the home.[5] Therefore, addressing barriers to WSMEs, especially access to finance, is a direct path to achieving gender equality, poverty reduction, and inclusive socioeconomic growth. In the same World Bank report, Viet Nam ranks 97th on composite indicators of Women, Business, and Law, with a score of 79. Other barriers include gender-based violence (GBV) and time constraints due to the unequal gendered distribution of household responsibilities and unpaid care work. Gender norms restrict both men and women, but in Viet Nam, women disproportionately bear the burden of inequality. Meanwhile, policymakers, business support organizations, banks, and other financial institutions are constrained by a lack of accurate data and meaningful

---

[1] In this document, SMEs in Viet Nam also include microenterprises. See Appendix 1 for a detailed definition.
[2] General Statistics Office (GSO). 2021. *Viet Nam Economic Census*. Ha Noi: Viet Nam.
[3] GSO. White Book on Enterprise 2022 (p. 91).
[4] Alliance for Financial Inclusion (AFI). 2021. *A Policy Framework for Women-Led MSME Access to Finance*. Kuala Lumpur. p. 5.
[5] Footnote 3, p. 3.

disaggregation by gender, age, and (dis)ability. This has typically made it difficult to determine the specific needs and characteristics of women-owned enterprises and develop targeted marketing strategies for this segment.

Given the COVID-19 pandemic and the continued recovery across the globe, it is important to understand the obstacles that women and their businesses encounter in Viet Nam. According to a growing body of literature, WSMEs were disproportionately affected and more likely to close during the first year of the pandemic.[6] With schools closed and students transitioning to online learning, women who served as childcare providers faced increased pressure. They were more likely to go out for groceries and other essential household tasks, increasing their risk of infection. The impact of nationwide lockdowns only served to exacerbate the issues of gender-based and household violence. While often sharing the same obstacles to growth as those experienced by men-owned businesses, discriminatory practices and internalized gender biases mean that WSMEs encounter barriers to a greater degree. Crucially, internalized social norms and self-selection biases are typically manifested from a very young age in Viet Nam. Despite a constitutionally mandated recognition of gender equality and increasing legal and regulatory amendments to uphold gender equality, women entrepreneurs live with norms and social values that reinforce the subordination of women.[7]

The Asian Development Bank (ADB) is implementing the Women Accelerating Vibrant Enterprises in Southeast Asia and the Pacific (WAVES) program funded by the Women Entrepreneurs Finance Initiative (We-Fi), which aims to support women-owned SMEs to access financing and training in Viet Nam and the Pacific. The White Book, the first of its kind, has been produced under Component 2 of the WAVES program, Technical Assistance 9660 (Regional): Promoting Transformative Gender Equality Agenda in Asia and the Pacific. It provides comprehensive insights into the challenges and opportunities faced by SMEs, particularly those owned by women, and provides recommendations for policymakers on how to effectively support the development of WSMEs. It is expected that the study will serve as a foundation for future research and policymaking initiatives aimed at fostering the growth and development of the SME sector.

This White Book uses the SME definition in the 2017 Law on SME Support that encompasses micro, small, and medium-sized enterprises. It makes extensive use of data from the GSO 2021 Economic Census—the first ever WSME database collected nationwide with support from We-Fi and ADB and technical guidance provided by the Agency for Enterprise Development (AED), Ministry of Planning and Development (MPI) under this project. Questionnaire 1.15 (Q1.15) was included in the census to ask about WSMEs only. Additionally, the study builds from existing literature, policy and regulatory framework reviews, a barrier study alongside further surveys, interviews, consultations with WSMEs, Viet Nam Women's Union, business associations, and other stakeholders across four

---

[6] Katie Sproule and Nguyen Thanh Huong. 2021. *USAID/Vietnam COVID-Specific Gender Analysis.* Prepared by Banyan Global.

[7] As defined under the Law on Gender Equality 2006, "Gender equality indicates that men and women have equal positions and roles; are given equal conditions and opportunities to develop their capacities for the development of the community and family, and equally enjoy the achievement of that development."

provinces, including Lao Cai (Northern Region), Thua Thien Hue (Central Region), Lam Dong (Central Highlands), and Can Tho (Southern Region). The report analyzes only active enterprises to provide an up-to-date picture of the WSMEs.

The gender-disaggregated data from the census provides a unique value-add for this first White Book about women doing business in Viet Nam. It allows for the focus to be on the data surrounding gender-specific issues in business. One limitation, however, was that data on state support to dynamic SMEs (Q1.15 of this census) was only asked of WSMEs, so the data cannot be compared to men-owned SMEs.[8] A further limitation is that this census data gives measures of outcomes possibly due to bias and discrimination, but it does not offer any insights or does it measure bias and discrimination per se. For example, that only 20% of SMEs are owned by women suggests bias and supports "there is bias" assertions, but it is not a measure of general, let alone particular, biases. In Chapter 4, which presents a typology of forms of bias, the discussion is supplemented with a modest survey of 118 WSMEs who report their perceptions about which are important or not. The budget and COVID-19 pandemic context limited the sample size, which should be bigger and include men-owned SMEs in the next White Book. That small sample is, nevertheless, the only data that provides insight into which forms of bias are most important. More quantitative research is required in this area.

The report is structured as follows: Chapter 1 is an overview of the White Book report, delineating its framework and organization. Chapter 2 presents an overview of women's entrepreneurship alongside gender statistics and a situational analysis of Vietnamese business ownership and characteristics in relation to others in Southeast Asia and beyond. Chapter 3 provides an overview of WSMEs in Viet Nam. Chapter 4 summarizes the main gendered barriers facing WSMEs. Chapter 5 provides a review of the legal and policy framework governing WSMEs at the provincial and central levels. Chapters 4 and 5 both include discussions on the implications of COVID-19 and the effectiveness of policy responses. Chapter 6 gives a summary of international good practice, and the report concludes with a set of targeted policy recommendations.

---

[8]   Q1.15 is summarized in Appendix 2.

Women Entrepreneurship in Viet Nam and Abroad: An International Comparison

This chapter presents an international and regional comparison of women's entrepreneurship in Viet Nam to other economies. Overall, Viet Nam performs relatively well on measures of gender equality, particularly regarding the legal and regulatory environment.

Women Entrepreneurship in Viet Nam and Abroad

Women own only about 1-in-4 Vietnamese businesses, but this proportion compares well with many other economies.[9] According to the Mastercard Index of Women Entrepreneurs (MIWE) published in 2020, Viet Nam ranks 23rd in its share of women as a percentage of business owners out of the 58 economies selected for the assessment. In Viet Nam, 26.5% of business owners are women, and this compares favorably to other economies in the region (Thailand 23%; Indonesia 21%; and Singapore 24%). Globally, Viet Nam scores well against economies such as France (24%), and Sweden (20%). However, it ranks behind economies such as Ghana (36%), Malawi (31%), and the Philippines (27%).[10]

Data on entrepreneurial activity suggests a leading role for young women. Of those engaging in early stage entrepreneurial activity, there are more women than men: higher than in more developed economies such as Israel and the United States (US) (Figure 1).[11]

Women are also strongly represented in the overall formal labor force. Sixty-eight percent of women aged 15+ participated in the labor force in 2021 (73% in rural and 61% in urban areas) compared to 57% in the US, 66% in New Zealand, 52% in Indonesia, and 44% in the Philippines. In terms of access to education, the level of attainment is little different between men and women (ILO 2021) although girls have a higher secondary school completion rate than boys (UNICEF 2021).[12]

---

[9] The MIWE reported 26.5% women-owned enterprises in Viet Nam (about 1-in-4), while the 2021 Census, using a different definition and data source, showed 20% of SMEs were women-owned. This chapter refers to 26.5% to make it methodologically consistent for cross-economy comparisons, but other chapters use the 2021 Census data, unless otherwise stated.

[10] *The Mastercard Index of Women Entrepreneurs 2020 Report.*

[11] The labor force participation rate here refers to the percentage of women aged 15+ that participated in the workforce.

[12] Source: ILOSTAT database (accessed January 2023).

Figure 1: Female–Male Ratio of Total Early Stage Entrepreneurial Activity

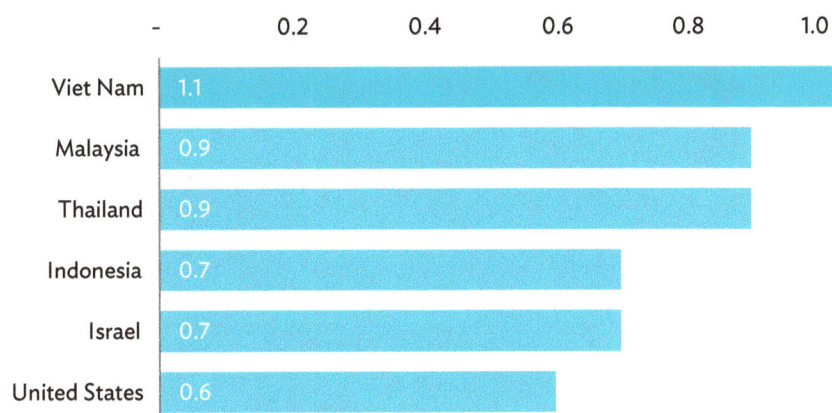

	-	0.2	0.4	0.6	0.8	1.0
Viet Nam	1.1					
Malaysia	0.9					
Thailand	0.9					
Indonesia	0.7					
Israel	0.7					
United States	0.6					

Note: Total Early-stage Entrepreneurial Activity – TEA - Percentage of the adult population between the ages of 18 and 64 years who are in the process of starting a business or already started a business (a nascent entrepreneur or owner-manager of a new business) which is less than 42 months old.
Source: Global Entrepreneurship Monitor, 2017.

Nevertheless, there remains strong evidence that women are still subject to barriers in business (Chapter 4). The proportion of women in managerial positions was only 25% in 2021. The proportion of women in senior and middle-management positions fell from 23% in 2020 to 16% in 2021.[13] These percentages are similar to those in regional economies, although they are higher in many other economies globally.

Legal and Regulatory Framework

Viet Nam's legal framework is comprehensive in enabling women to participate in the wider economy. Law No. 73/2006/QH11 dated 29 November 2006 on gender equality came into effect in 2007 and mandates government bodies to fulfill their responsibilities on gender equality and to address violations. In addition, the law outlines numerous protections for women that are not common in other economies within the region or globally. Notably, Viet Nam mandates equal pay for work of equal value, unlike Indonesia, Malaysia, and Singapore. Additionally, in surpassing the International Labour Organization's (ILO's) minimum recommendation of 14 weeks, Viet Nam has among the highest allowances for paid maternity leave in the selected sample (Table 1).

---

[13]   Source: ILOSTAT database (accessed January 2023).

Table 1: Legal Protections by Economy

Item	Indonesia	Malaysia	Singapore	Thailand	Viet Nam
Does the law prohibit discrimination in employment based on gender?	Yes	No	No	Yes	Yes
Does the law mandate equal remuneration for work of equal value?	No	No	No	Yes	Yes
Is paid leave of at least 14 weeks available to mothers?	No	No	Yes	No	Yes
Length of paid maternity leave (days)	90	60	84	90	180
Does the government administer 100% of maternity leave benefits?	No	No	No	No	Yes
Is dismissal of pregnant workers prohibited?	Yes	No	No	Yes	Yes
Does the law prohibit discrimination in access to credit based on gender?	Yes	Yes	Yes	Yes	Yes
Can a woman register a business in the same way as a man?	Yes	Yes	Yes	Yes	Yes
Are the ages at which men and women can retire with full pension benefits equal?	Yes	Yes	Yes	Yes	No
Retirement age of women	58	60	63 (mandatory)	55	56 (mandatory)
Retirement age of men	58	60	63 (mandatory)	55	61 (mandatory)

Source: The World Bank Gender Data Portal, Trading Economics.

Gender Gap Indicators

Although more needs to be done to track the implementation of laws on gender equality, early evidence suggests that the effects have been broadly positive in creating opportunities for entrepreneurship among women. Figure 2 compares the Mastercard Index of Women Entrepreneurs' data on the share of women-owned businesses with the Women, Business, and Law (WBL) index created by the World Bank.[14] A high WBL score is positively correlated to a higher percentage of women business owners. Economies that have formal legal discrimination

---

14   The WBL methodology is not particularly complex and Viet Nam would score near 100 points were it not for the different retirement ages for men and women.

against women (e.g., Iran) tend to have women owning less than 10% of businesses. Compared to other Asian economies, Viet Nam is higher on both measures. Being higher does not seem to be necessarily related to being a rich economy.

The data in Figure 2 presents a consistent story that, by available cross-economy measures, women doing business in Viet Nam have stronger legal protections than in many regional economies. Consequently, women participate actively in the workforce and, by global standards, have a notable minority role in political leadership and business ownership. There is no obvious explanation, therefore, as to why Vietnamese women own only 20%–25% of SMEs. In the next chapter, using the recent economic census data, the nature and the differences between WSMEs and men-owned SMEs are analyzed to better understand barriers and challenges faced by WSMEs.

Figure 2: Women, Business, and Law Index and Share of Women-Owned Businesses (%)

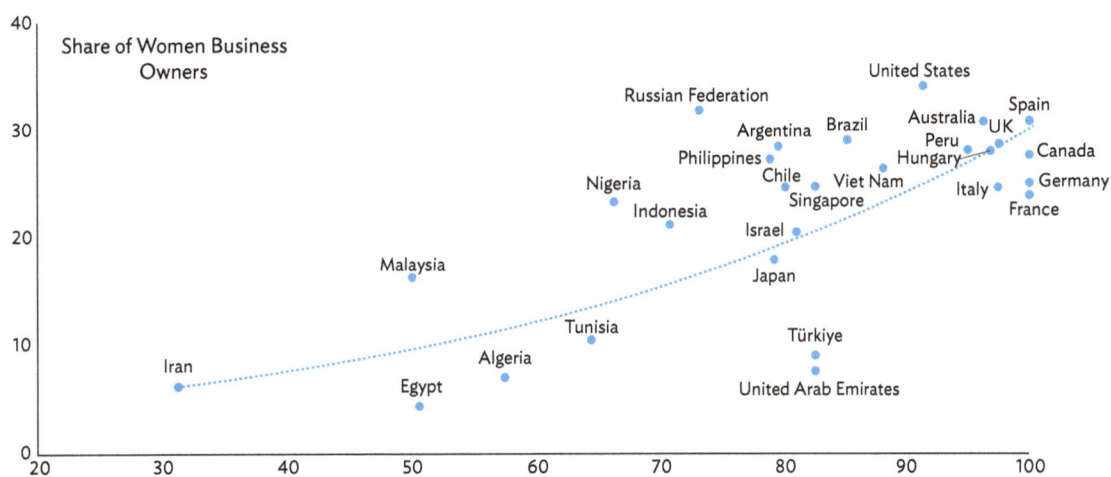

UK = United Kingdom.

Note: The WBL Score is a composite measure of eight factors organized around women's interactions with the law: Mobility, Workplace, Pay, Marriage, Parenthood, Entrepreneurship, Assets, and Pension.

Source: Mastercard Index of Women Entrepreneurs. 2020. World Bank, Women, Business, and the Law (2023).

Overview of Women-Owned Small and Medium-Sized Enterprises in Viet Nam

3

This chapter analyzes WSMEs by size, location, and sector, and their needs for support and capacity using the data from the 2021 Economic Census of the General Statistics Office (GSO) of Viet Nam.[15] This report focuses on active SMEs and WSMEs only, and the tables in this section are not exhaustive. Only selected regions and sectors are discussed.

Women-Owned Small and Medium-Sized Enterprises in Viet Nam

As of 31 December 2020, there were 540,909 "active" enterprises in Viet Nam, of which 523,124 were SMEs. Women owned 105,876 (20%) of the active SMEs (Table 2).

Table 2: Active Enterprises as of 31 December 2020

Item	SMEs				WSMEs			
	Micro	Small	Medium	Total	Micro	Small	Medium	Total
Whole country	478,601	163,760	23,895	**666,256**	94,581	29,828	3,589	**127,998**
Of which, active only	340,900	158,670	23,554	**523,124**	72,874	29,425	3,577	**105,876**
Of which, active only (%)	71	97	99	**79**	77	99	100	**83**

SMEs = small and medium-sized enterprises, WSMEs = women-owned small and medium-sized enterprises.
Source: General Statistics Office. 2021. Economic Census.

According to the definitions in the SME Support Law (Appendix 1), two-thirds of Vietnamese SMEs were of "micro," and fewer than 5% were of "medium" size. On average, WSMEs were smaller than men-owned SMEs (e.g., only 3% of the WSMEs were medium). Seventy-one percent of SMEs (and 72% of WSMEs) are in two of Viet Nam's six regions: the Red River Delta (the north) and the South East (the south). Although there are more SMEs in the South East, the average

---

[15] 2021 Census figures as of 31 December 2020.

size of SMEs in the Red River Delta is slightly larger. Forty-four percent of WSMEs operated in the wholesale and retail trade sector (Table 3).

While WSMEs are only 20% of all SMEs, they are 37% of all SMEs in the education and training sector (e.g., running private pre-schools) and 31% of all in the accommodation and food services. WSMEs were notably underrepresented in construction (10%), and mining and quarrying (12%) (Table 4).

Table 3: Small and Medium-Sized Enterprises: Size, Location, and Sector

Item	Men-Owned SMEs				WSMEs			
	Micro	Small	Medium	Total	Micro	Small	Medium	Total
All Viet Nam (number)	268,026	129,245	19,977	417,248	72,874	29,425	3,577	105,876
All Viet Nam (%)	64	31	5		69	28	3	
By location								
Red River Delta	61	34	5	**137,278**	66	30	4	**31,057**
South East	67	28	5	**158,742**	71	26	3	**45,337**
Mekong River Delta	67	29	4	**33,159**	67	29	4	**8,767**
By sector								
Agriculture, forestry, and fishing	53	39	8	**3,448**	49	48	3	**673**
Mining and quarrying	34	56	10	**1,972**	38	54	8	**267**
Manufacturing	48	42	10	**67,136**	51	42	7	**14,466**
Electricity, gas, stream, and air conditioning supply	66	24	10	**2,713**	77	18	5	**537**
Water supply, sewerage, waste management, and remediation activities	54	39	7	**1,712**	69	28	3	**331**
Construction	49	45	6	**64,648**	51	44	5	**7,099**
Wholesale and retail trade; repair of motor vehicles and motorcycles	70	27	3	**155,216**	70	27	3	**49,055**
Of which, wholesale and retail trade	71	26	3	**145,839**	70	27	3	**47,028**
Transportation and storage	66	30	4	**25,234**	72	26	2	**6,752**
Accommodation and food service activities	79	19	2	**13,165**	84	15	1	**5,977**
Information and communication	72	24	4	**9,468**	80	18	2	**1,562**
Financial, banking, and insurance activities	71	24	5	**1,608**	76	22	2	**632**

continued on next page

Item	Men-Owned SMEs				WSMEs			
	Micro	Small	Medium	Total	Micro	Small	Medium	Total
Real estate activities	68	26	6	**9,359**	76	21	3	**2,296**
Professional, scientific, and technical activities	79	19	2	**36,421**	84	15	1	**7,157**
Administrative and support service activities	77	19	4	**15,470**	82	16	2	**4,842**
Education and training	70	25	5	**3,844**	71	25	4	**2,283**
Human health and social work activities	53	38	9	**1,569**	56	36	8	**540**
Arts, entertainment, and recreation	80	17	3	**1,717**	83	14	3	**530**
Other service activities	85	14	1	**2,548**	88	11	1	**877**

WSMEs = women-owned small and medium-sized enterprises.
Source: General Statistics Office. 2021. Economic Census.

Table 4: Proportion of Women-Owned Small and Medium-Sized Enterprises in Each Industry (%)

Sector	Proportion
All Viet Nam	**20**
Agriculture, forestry, and fishing	16
Mining and quarrying	12
Manufacturing	18
Electricity, gas, stream, and air conditioning supply	17
Water supply, sewerage, waste management, and remediation activities	16
Construction	10
Wholesale and retail trade; repair of motor vehicles and motorcycles	24
Of which, wholesale and retail trade	24
Transportation and storage	21
Accommodation and food service activities	31
Information and communication	14
Financial, banking, and insurance activities	28
Real estate activities	20
Professional, scientific, and technical activities	16
Administrative and support service activities	24
Education and training	37
Human health and social work activities	26
Arts, entertainment, and recreation	24
Other service activities	26

Source: General Statistics Office. 2021. Economic Census.

SMEs are typically private limited companies (71% of all men-owned SMEs are private limited company), although 20% of men-owned SMEs were joint-stock companies (compared to only 12% of WSMEs). Interestingly, the joint-stock form was much more common in the north (36% of men-owned SMEs and 25% of WSMEs) than in the south (12% of men-owned SMEs, and 7% of WSMEs). Joint-stock companies were proportionally most frequent in three sectors: wholesale and retail trade, construction, and manufacturing (Table 5).

Table 5: Main Forms of Legal Incorporation for Small and Medium-Sized Enterprises

Item	Men-Owned SMEs (of 417,248)		WSMEs (of 105,876)	
	Private Limited Company with Zero State Capital or ≤ 50%	Joint-Stock Company without State Capital	Private Limited Company with Zero State Capital or ≤ 50%	Joint-Stock Company without State Capital
All Viet Nam	**296,018**	**85,065**	**84,481**	**13,047**
By region				
Red River Delta	80,520	48,888	22,329	7,862
South East	127,946	18,392	39,670	2,989
Mekong River Delta	23,250	2,277	6,120	329
By sector				
Agriculture, forestry, and fishing	2,058	640	420	101
Mining and quarrying	1,226	609	181	57
Manufacturing	47,907	11,105	12,065	1,549
Electricity, gas, stream, and air conditioning supply	1,517	931	405	78
Water supply, sewerage, waste management, and remediation activities	1,076	451	260	40
Construction	45,065	17,610	5,621	1,336
Wholesale and retail trade; repair of motor vehicles and motorcycles	116,933	23,916	39,672	4,735
Of which, wholesale and retail trade	109,368	22,629	37,944	4,569
Transportation and storage	19,737	4,034	5,768	686
Accommodation and food service activities	9,556	1,788	4,640	463
Information and communication	5,120	3,189	1,146	369
Financial, banking, and insurance activities	1,000	367	508	66
Real estate activities	4,525	3,917	1,487	622
Professional, scientific, and technical activities	22,512	10,596	5,324	1,323
Administrative and support service activities	11,122	3,604	3,829	840
Education and training	2,339	1,215	1,585	536
Human health and social work activities	1,061	429	412	117
Arts, entertainment, and recreation	1,225	334	407	60
Other service activities	2,039	330	751	69

WSMEs = women-owned small and medium-sized enterprises.
Source: General Statistics Office. 2021. Economic Census.

The GSO Economic Census collected many useful data that helps reveal the nature of Vietnamese SMEs. Almost one-quarter of all SMEs surveyed reported having their own website (over 20% in most industries), and more than two-thirds have business loans requiring regular interest repayments. These proportions are almost the same for men-owned SMEs and WSMEs. Websites were much more common with northern SMEs than in the south, although the SMEs in the South East were marginally more likely to borrow with interest (Table 6). This suggests that while most SMEs may be modest operations with little ambition or use of technologies, a significant number is "dynamic" and seeking to learn and grow.[16]

Table 6: Identifying "Dynamic" Small and Medium-Sized Enterprises
(%)

Item	Have a Website		Have Loan Interest Expenses	
	Men-Owned SMEs	WSMEs	Men-Owned SMEs	WSMEs
All Viet Nam	**25**	**22**	**69**	**68**
By region				
Red River Delta	35	32	71	69
South East	24	21	75	75
Mekong River Delta	11	10	54	53
By sector				
Agriculture, forestry, and fishing	20	18	63	63
Mining and quarrying	15	13	65	64
Manufacturing	26	23	70	69
Electricity, gas, stream, and air conditioning supply	10	7	70	66
Water supply, sewerage, waste management, and remediation activities	24	17	69	69
Construction	22	19	68	67
Wholesale and retail trade; repair of motor vehicles and motorcycles	23	21	70	69
Of which, wholesale and retail trade	23	21	69	69
Transportation and storage	22	22	72	72
Accommodation and food service activities	22	20	66	65
Information and communication	44	35	68	67
Financial, banking, and insurance activities	30	19	57	57

continued on next page

---

[16] "Dynamic" is a loose definition based on what measures of the more interesting and innovative WSMEs are available. At first glance, they are just WSMEs with loans or websites, but then value-chains and other features are added. This subsection is based on the data from Questionnaire 1.15 of the 2021 Economic Census, which was asked of all WSMEs but not men-owned SMEs. In Table 6, the concept of dynamic SMEs was introduced, with some proxy indicators of having a website and paying interest on one or more loans. Questionnaire 1.15 in the Census takes the dynamic concept further by identifying WSMEs participating in supply chains or value chains, having branded or certified products, undertaking innovation, digital transformation activities, or actively strengthening human resources.

Table 6 *continued*

Item	Have a Website		Have Loan Interest Expenses	
	Men-Owned SMEs	WSMEs	Men-Owned SMEs	WSMEs
Real estate activities	30	25	72	72
Professional, scientific, and technical activities	27	26	67	68
Administrative and support service activities	29	27	69	67
Education and training	36	32	65	62
Human health and social work activities	30	32	67	68
Arts, entertainment, and recreation	23	22	67	63
Other service activities	22	20	65	66

WSMEs = women-owned small and medium-sized enterprises.

Source: General Statistics Office. 2021. Economic Census.

Despite the COVID-19 pandemic, many SMEs did grow in 2020, at least in terms of the number of employees. Overall, both men-owned SMEs and WSMEs increased their total number of employees by 3% by year-end in 2020 (Table 7). Broken down by size, however, all the growth was in SMEs, with even small falls in employment by microenterprises. Northern SMEs, particularly northern WSMEs, grew stronger than those in the south. The sector breakdown shows a mixed growth story. The accommodation and food sector shed many workers, although this was balanced out by strong job growth in electricity, gas, stream, air conditioning supply, construction, and education and training sectors.

Another interesting finding, consistent across all Viet Nam from the north to the south, is that women employ more women (particularly in micro WSMEs) (as seen in Table 7). While women may only own 20% of SMEs, they comprise over 38% of the SME workforce. As may be expected, the percentage of women employees varies across sectors, being lowest in mining and quarrying, and construction and highest in education and training (Table 7).

There are many more financial data questions in the GSO Economic Census, but such reporting is notoriously biased (e.g., 49% of men-owned SMEs and 52% of WSMEs reported making net losses in 2020 despite an overall increase in employment by SMEs). Furthermore, 2020 was a COVID year, so financial data does not reflect "normal business." Nevertheless, in Tables 8 and 9, financial data concerning employees, taxes paid, and total revenues are presented.

Table 7: Identifying "Dynamic" Small and Medium-Sized Enterprises (%)

Item	Change in Number of Employees at Year End Compared to Year Start								Women Employees at Year End							
	Men-Owned SMEs				WSMEs				Men-Owned SMEs				WSMEs			
	Micro	Small	Med	Total	Micro	Small	Med	Total	Micro	Small	Med	Total	Micro	Small	Med	Total
All Viet Nam	**(2)**	**5**	**4**	**3**	**(1)**	**5**	**5**	**3**	**34**	**35**	**37**	**35**	**56**	**45**	**46**	**48**
By region																
Red River Delta	(1)	6	5	**4**	1	7	12	**6**	37	38	39	38	58	49	50	**52**
South East	(1)	4	3	**2**	(1)	4	2	**2**	33	35	39	36	58	45	45	**49**
Mekong River Delta	(1)	2	1	**1**	0	3	(2)	**1**	28	27	35	29	44	35	44	**40**
By sector																
Agriculture, forestry, and fishing	(2)	1	1	**1**	(7)	(1)	1	**(1)**	33	25	34	29	50	22	23	**26**
Mining and quarrying	(11)	2	2	**1**	(8)	9	(17)	**(2)**	24	21	21	21	36	24	25	**26**
Manufacturing	(6)	2	2	**1**	(5)	3	2	**2**	32	42	46	43	54	51	52	**52**
Electricity, gas, stream, and air conditioning supply	55	17	10	**21**	64	40	7	**38**	25	19	18	20	46	26	25	**34**
Water supply, sewerage, waste management, and remediation activities	1	7	1	**4**	5	7	11	**7**	30	35	34	34	46	44	43	**44**
Construction	(6)	10	11	**8**	(4)	12	23	**12**	23	21	21	22	42	25	23	**27**
Wholesale and retail trade; repair of motor vehicles and motorcycles	2	6	6	**5**	3	7	5	**5**	37	39	38	38	57	46	45	**50**
Of which, wholesale and retail trade	2	7	5	**5**	3	7	4	**5**	38	39	39	38	57	46	45	**50**

continued on next page

Table 7 continued

| Item | Change in Number of Employees at Year End Compared to Year Start | | | | | | | | Women Employees at Year End | | | | | | | |
| | Men-Owned SMEs | | | | WSMEs | | | | Men-Owned SMEs | | | | WSMEs | | | |
	Micro	Small	Med	Total	Micro	Small	Med	Total	Micro	Small	Med	Total	Micro	Small	Med	Total
Transportation and storage	(1)	1	3	**1**	0	5	(5)	**2**	28	25	25	26	45	30	28	**35**
Accommodation and food service activities	(19)	(17)	(18)	**(18)**	(16)	(11)	(10)	**(13)**	49	51	52	51	62	53	52	**57**
Information and communication	(1)	9	15	**8**	1	8	16	**7**	34	37	36	36	57	45	42	**49**
Financial, banking, and insurance activities	2	16	(20)	**(0)**	5	8	15	**8**	50	56	55	54	70	65	57	**66**
Real estate activities	(8)	4	2	**0**	(8)	5	9	**1**	40	41	38	40	59	49	37	**50**
Professional, scientific, and technical activities	(1)	9	12	**5**	1	12	29	**8**	34	34	37	34	58	48	44	**52**
Administrative and support service activities	(11)	(3)	3	**(4)**	(9)	1	8	**(2)**	38	36	29	35	60	43	39	**49**
Education and training	3	9	10	**8**	5	12	15	**11**	55	68	62	63	77	76	72	**75**
Human health and social work activities	3	9	6	**7**	12	13	7	**11**	52	59	63	60	68	64	66	**65**
Arts, entertainment, and recreation	(5)	(2)	1	**(2)**	(1)	(3)	6	**0**	40	44	40	42	58	51	58	**55**
Other service activities	(6)	7	(16)	**(3)**	(7)	(1)	14	**(2)**	38	44	38	41	71	61	63	**66**

( ) = negative, Med = medium, WSMEs = women-owned small and medium-sized enterprises.
Source: General Statistics Office. 2021. Economic Census.

Table 8: Average Amount Paid per Employee in 2020
(D million)

Item	Men-Owned SMEs				WSMEs			
	Micro	Small	Med	Total	Micro	Small	Med	Total
All Viet Nam	**63**	**94**	**112**	**93**	**59**	**87**	**98**	**81**
By region								
Red River Delta	67	97	113	**95**	63	90	99	**84**
South East	69	110	133	**108**	66	99	113	**93**
Mekong River Delta	51	75	97	**75**	46	70	81	**66**
By sector								
Agriculture, forestry, and fishing	49	81	85	**79**	53	80	72	**75**
Mining and quarrying	56	78	105	**86**	42	80	110	**84**
Manufacturing	55	86	108	**93**	56	81	96	**83**
Electricity, gas, stream, and air conditioning supply	53	91	138	**102**	33	74	103	**64**
Water supply, sewerage, waste management, and remediation activities	59	90	110	**94**	52	75	82	**70**
Construction	59	84	93	**83**	57	79	78	**75**
Wholesale and retail trade; repair of motor vehicles and motorcycles	58	97	122	**86**	55	90	110	**80**
Of which, wholesale and retail trade	59	97	125	**87**	55	91	111	**80**
Transportation and storage	69	102	122	**97**	67	95	105	**87**
Accommodation and food service activities	53	70	82	**66**	51	63	76	**59**
Information and communication	99	177	204	**166**	87	135	198	**130**
Financial, banking, and insurance activities	95	150	364	**197**	74	110	102	**95**
Real estate activities	79	129	150	**123**	75	117	144	**107**
Professional, scientific, and technical activities	79	135	175	**119**	73	120	119	**97**
Administrative and support service activities	65	96	94	**86**	64	89	84	**79**
Education and training	63	86	94	**83**	58	73	91	**74**
Human health and social work activities	69	85	113	**93**	66	82	100	**86**
Arts, entertainment, and recreation	57	93	121	**89**	51	94	67	**71**
Other service activities	55	75	93	**69**	49	71	105	**65**

Med = medium, WSMEs = women-owned small and medium-sized enterprises.
Source: General Statistics Office. 2021. Economic Census.

The average salary paid to employees increased with the size of the enterprise, with medium SMEs paying, on average, higher employee remuneration. WSMEs paid their employees less than men-owned SMEs, particularly medium SMEs (Table 8). This is a matter for further research, but the characteristics of WSMEs would explain most of the difference (smaller enterprises, less capital-intensive sectors, etc.). Similarly, that average WSMEs are paying notably lower total taxes than men-owned SMEs, while having slightly higher reported 2020 revenues, needs investigation (Table 9).

The above analysis shows that Vietnamese women own, by global standards, a significant share of SMEs and are 38% of the SME workforce. It also seems that women own and run somewhat smaller SMEs than do men and tend to concentrate in less capital-intensive sectors and more in the traditional education and training sector. There are also differences between the nature of WSMEs in the north and south of Viet Nam that warrant further research.

By disaggregating the data by size, sector, and location, this chapter has provided an overview of the situation for WSMEs in Viet Nam. In doing so, it has emphasized some of the main differences between men-owned and WSMEs and raised questions about the causes of these differences. Chapter 4 provides some possible answers to these questions by examining the barriers to growth and development faced by WSMEs in Viet Nam.

Table 9: Financial Performance of Small and Medium-Sized Enterprises
(D million)

| Item | Average Taxes and Other Payables to State per Enterprise | | | | | | | | Average Net Revenue from Sales of Goods and Provision of Services per Enterprise | | | | | | | |
| | Men-Owned SMEs | | | | WSMEs | | | | Men-Owned SMEs | | | | WSMEs | | | |
	Micro	Small	Med	Total	Micro	Small	Med	Total	Micro	Small	Med	Total	Micro	Small	Med	Total
All Viet Nam	**27**	**182**	**903**	**117**	**20**	**132**	**432**	**65**	**1,952**	**22,392**	**110,341**	**13,473**	**2,038**	**26,414**	**125,570**	**12,986**
By region																
Red River Delta	30	175	847	**123**	19	129	304	**64**	1,869	21,952	109,369	**14,426**	2,038	25,811	128,200	**14,231**
South East	22	166	767	**97**	21	126	514	**64**	1,872	24,357	114,338	**13,370**	1,921	26,050	123,395	**12,051**
Mekong River Delta	32	142	818	**98**	21	190	478	**86**	2,453	26,738	123,895	**14,773**	2,628	31,481	139,800	**15,917**
By sector																
Agriculture, forestry, and fishing	33	142	891	**141**	8	48	300	**36**	1,018	13,590	80,684	**12,051**	1,036	15,060	115,863	**11,500**
Mining and quarrying	245	845	4,756	**1,038**	77	655	1,045	**466**	1,280	14,300	97,862	**18,347**	1,478	14,001	106,222	**16,816**
Manufacturing	15	119	503	**108**	13	106	313	**74**	1,185	14,302	95,197	**16,328**	1,177	14,155	94,980	**13,697**
Electricity, gas, stream, and air conditioning supply	69	356	2,750	**402**	5	118	2,143	**129**	778	13,385	118,501	**15,401**	615	11,373	103,552	**7,502**
Water supply, sewerage, waste management, and remediation activities	14	147	797	**121**	11	99	1,317	**67**	850	12,700	87,269	**11,598**	810	9,091	67,918	**4,784**
Construction	37	206	890	**164**	25	146	429	**100**	1,168	12,555	83,391	**11,192**	1,213	12,812	79,659	**10,440**
Wholesale and retail trade; repair of motor vehicles and motorcycles	17	125	575	**62**	14	90	335	**43**	2,826	39,304	191,518	**18,008**	2,841	40,909	193,107	**18,374**
Of which, wholesale and retail trade	17	127	545	61	14	78	348	40	2,862	39,192	188,319	17,810	2,837	40,683	193,439	18,161

continued on next page

Table 9 *continued*

| Item | Average Taxes and Other Payables to State per Enterprise | | | | | | | | Average Net Revenue from Sales of Goods and Provision of Services per Enterprise | | | | | | | |
| | Men-Owned SMEs | | | | WSMEs | | | | Men-Owned SMEs | | | | WSMEs | | | |
	Micro	Small	Med	Total	Micro	Small	Med	Total	Micro	Small	Med	Total	Micro	Small	Med	Total
Transportation and storage	27	169	818	98	24	122	553	61	2,326	24,524	106,043	12,682	2,528	23,931	133,828	11,097
Accommodation and food service activities	20	150	541	57	47	94	470	59	1,379	12,426	44,883	4,553	1,145	13,113	41,037	3,466
Information and communication	21	223	883	106	18	185	882	67	1,318	15,135	56,040	6,922	1,351	18,239	64,527	5,802
Financial, banking and insurance activities	44	284	620	130	19	165	2,029	86	1,283	16,678	121,149	10,896	1,191	8,324	59,482	3,797
Real estate activities	186	1,134	6,929	810	91	1,449	2,083	441	1,798	22,827	119,084	13,825	1,657	21,610	116,020	9,328
Professional, scientific, and technical activities	32	262	1,220	96	25	188	996	59	1,256	12,368	61,382	4,426	1,108	13,238	55,320	3,416
Administrative and support service activities	28	187	973	92	22	148	290	48	1,390	13,370	35,888	4,907	1,287	13,645	42,406	4,176
Education and training	15	74	217	39	7	87	716	55	595	5,017	18,449	2,550	498	4,383	15,515	2,045
Human health and social work activities	6	45	218	40	4	53	94	29	871	8,404	33,538	6,619	748	6,520	18,053	4,242
Arts, entertainment, and recreation	24	400	2,689	171	19	139	316	44	949	16,265	69,153	5,668	741	9,514	29,235	2,756
Other service activities	12	133	701	38	10	49	823	23	901	11,927	51,575	3,105	666	7,237	67,247	2,129

Med = medium, WSMEs = women-owned small and medium-sized enterprises.
Source: General Statistics Office. 2021. Economic Census.

State Support for Dynamic Women-Owned Micro, Small, and Medium-Sized Enterprises

This section is based on the data from Questionnaire 1.15 of the 2021 Economic Census, which was asked of all WSMEs but not men-owned SMEs. In Table 6, the concept of "dynamic" SMEs was introduced, with some proxy indicators of having a website and paying interest on one or more loans. Questionnaire 1.15 takes the dynamic concept further by identifying WSMEs participating in supply chains or value chains, having branded or certified products, undertaking innovation or digital transformation activities, or actively strengthening human resources, all factors that are critical to WSMEs consolidation and scaling up. The vast majority of WSMEs, however, are not dynamic in this sense. They are simply doing business day-to-day, without expansion plans and relying on self-financing. That is to be expected. Dynamic WSMEs are a minority, but a significant minority for growth and modernization. This section examines the characteristics of these dynamic WSMEs and to what extent the state has been supporting them. As a result of not administering the questionnaire to men who own SMEs, comparable data for men-owned SMEs is unavailable.

Only 4% of all WSMEs reported they are active in supply and value chains, and of these, nearly half received at least one form of support from the state. The Red River Delta WSMEs received proportionately more support than the South East and the Mekong River Delta (probably linking agricultural food chains). Medium-sized WSMEs received somewhat more support than others. Support was also generally spread across sectors, although manufacturing WSMEs received slightly more. The most common forms of state support were business links, brand development, and standards and technical regulations (Table 10).

Only 3% of WSMEs had nationally branded products or services and 1% of WSMEs had internationally branded products or services (Table 11). The Red River Delta region (north) had more of these than the South East region (south). Some 6% of medium WSMEs had nationally branded products or services, and 2% of medium WSMEs had internationally branded products or services. Such brands were more frequent in the retail and wholesale trade sector. Certification was more common, with 10% of WSMEs having national or international product certifications. These were, again, more common with medium-size WSMEs (19%), and in the north compared to the south. National certifications were most common in manufacturing, although also high in trade, accommodation, and education sectors.

Table 10: Women-Owned Small and Medium-Sized Enterprises Active in Supply and Value Chains

Item	Number of WSMEs (Q 1.15)	Participating in Supply Chains, Industry Clusters, and Value Chains		WSMEs Participating in Supply Chains, Industry Clusters, and Value Chains Who Got at least One Type of State Support (Number)	WSMEs Participating in Supply Chains, Industry Clusters, and Value Chains Who Got at least One Type of State Support (%) Total	Number of WSMEs Participating in Supply Chains, Industry Clusters, and Value Chains by State Support Received						
		Number of WSMEs	Percentage (%)			Total	Subsidized Training Courses to Improve Technology, Specialized Production Techniques	Support for Production and Business Links	Support for Brand Development, Market Expansion	Consulting on Standards, Technical Regulations, Measurement, Quality	Support for Procedures for Production Testing, Verification, Inspection, and Quality Certification	Other
All WSMEs	**110,667**	**4,926**	**4**	**2,249**	**46**	**3,636**	**382**	**939**	**922**	**834**	**531**	**28**
By region												
Red River Delta	32,459	1,427	4	585	42	901	146	244	205	175	124	7
South East	47,238	1,411	3	562	40	897	95	194	235	214	151	8
Mekong River Delta	8,990	662	7	397	60	696	73	207	186	136	88	6
By size												
Medium	3,584	260	7	141	54	269	18	68	77	59	46	1
By sector												
Agriculture, forestry, and fishing	726	81	11	45	56	81	13	25	14	17	10	2
Mining and quarrying	289	19	7	5	26	6	0	2	2	1	1	0
Manufacturing	15,025	831	6	414	50	722	61	197	188	152	119	5
Electricity, gas, stream, and air conditioning supply	563	40	7	23	58	34	4	9	4	11	6	0
Water supply, sewerage, waste management, and remediation activities	341	10	3	4	40	7	2	0	0	1	3	1
Construction	7,441	341	5	153	45	247	31	60	46	72	38	0
Wholesale and retail trade; repair of motor vehicles and motorcycles	51,041	2,299	5	1,073	47	1,749	157	451	445	420	268	8

continued on next page

Table 10 continued

Item	Number of WSMEs (Q1.15)	Participating in Supply Chains, Industry Clusters, and Value Chains		WSMEs Participating in Supply Chains, Industry Clusters, and Value Chains Who Got at least One Type of State Support (Number)	WSMEs Participating in Supply Chains, Industry Clusters, and Value Chains Who Got at least One Type of State Support (%) Total	Number of WSMEs Participating in Supply Chains, Industry Clusters, and Value Chains by State Support Received					
		Number of WSMEs	Percentage (%)			Total	Subsidized Training Courses to Improve Technology, Specialized Production Techniques	Support for Production and Business Links	Support for Brand Development, Market Expansion	Consulting on Standards, Technical Regulations, Measurement, Quality	Support for Procedures for Production Testing, Verification, Inspection, and Quality Certification	Other
Of which, wholesale and retail trade	48,921	2,197	4	1,025	47	1,659	148	435	419	398	252	7
Transportation and storage	7,045	276	4	106	38	155	22	38	41	37	17	0
Accommodation and food service activities	6,372	251	4	116	46	177	24	45	52	32	21	3
Information and communication	1,639	69	4	23	33	40	5	11	9	9	6	0
Financial, banking, and insurance activities	670	46	7	24	52	37	6	7	18	4	2	0
Real estate activities	2,425	101	4	37	37	46	10	14	13	6	3	0
Professional, scientific, and technical activities	7,422	195	3	90	46	134	15	32	35	35	13	4
Administrative and support service activities	5,134	230	4	78	34	109	20	33	30	15	10	1
Education and training	2,466	78	3	31	40	44	7	5	10	13	7	2
Human health and social work activities	557	20	4	10	50	17	3	4	3	3	2	2
Arts, entertainment, and recreation	567	17	3	6	35	14	1	4	4	3	2	0
Other service activities	944	22	2	11	50	17	1	2	8	3	3	0

WSMEs = women-owned small and medium-sized enterprises.
Source: General Statistics Office. 2021. Economic Census.

Table 11: Branded and Certified Women–Owned Small and Medium–Sized Enterprises

Item	Number of WSMEs (Q 1.15)	Having National Branded Products or Services		Having International Branded Products or Services		Having Products Certified for National Product Quality		Having Products Certified for International Product Quality	
		Number of WSMEs	% of All WSMEs	Number of WSMEs	% of All WSMEs	Number of WSMEs	% of All WSMEs	Number of WSMEs	% of All WSMEs
All WSMEs	**110,667**	**2,984**	**3**	**849**	**1**	**9,457**	**9**	**1,102**	**1**
By region									
Red River Delta	32,459	968	3	342	1	3,072	9	452	1
South East	47,238	791	2	270	1	2,795	6	401	1
Mekong River Delta	8,990	306	3	33	0	1,078	12	45	1
By size									
Medium	3,584	201	6	54	2	590	16	98	3
By sector									
Agriculture, forestry, and fishing	726	32	4	3	0	98	13	5	1
Mining and quarrying	289	4	1	0	0	28	10	0	0
Manufacturing	15,025	450	3	52	0	1,658	11	129	1
Electricity, gas, stream, and air conditioning supply	563	9	2	0	0	45	8	0	0
Water supply, sewerage, waste management, and remediation activities	341	4	1	1	0	25	7	1	0
Construction	7,441	91	1	15	0	266	4	17	0
Wholesale and retail trade; repair of motor vehicles and motorcycles	51,041	1,934	4	643	1	5,535	11	795	2
Of which, wholesale and retail trade	48,921	1,829	4	588	1	5,327	11	749	2

continued on next page

Table 11 continued

Item	Number of WSMEs (Q 1.15)	Having National Branded Products or Services		Having International Branded Products or Services		Having Products Certified for National Product Quality		Having Products Certified for International Product Quality	
		Number of WSMEs	% of All WSMEs	Number of WSMEs	% of All WSMEs	Number of WSMEs	% of All WSMEs	Number of WSMEs	% of All WSMEs
Transportation and storage	7,045	70	1	19	0	171	2	21	0
Accommodation and food service activities	6,372	80	1	9	0	610	10	11	0
Information and communication	1,639	35	2	7	0	71	4	6	0
Financial, banking, and insurance activities	670	38	6	22	3	65	10	19	3
Real estate activities	2,425	25	1	5	0	56	2	2	0
Professional, scientific, and technical activities	7,422	69	1	20	0	286	4	26	0
Administrative and support service activities	5,134	52	1	14	0	192	4	23	0
Education and training	2,466	49	2	18	1	203	8	29	1
Human health and social work activities	557	20	4	5	1	88	16	7	1
Arts, entertainment, and recreation	567	8	1	3	1	14	2	3	1
Other service activities	944	14	1	13	1	46	5	8	1

WSMEs = women-owned small and medium-sized enterprises.

Source: General Statistics Office. 2021. Economic Census.

Table 12 shows the forms of brand development support given to WSMEs by the state. A total of 7,552 actions of assistance were given to 5,381 WSMEs (average 1.4 per WSME). While training was most common, support was spread fairly evenly across the five types. WSMEs in trade and manufacturing were the main beneficiaries.

Some 13,040 WSMEs (12%) reported undertaking business innovations, of whom 19% received one or more types of support from the state. Although medium-sized WSMEs were more likely to be innovating (26% were), they were only slightly more likely to have benefited from state support than other WSMEs. Once again, Mekong River WSMEs showed robust access to state support. Undertaking innovation varied across sectors (high in manufacturing and education), but support was fairly consistent across all sectors. Reading the six types of support provides an insight into how the state is supporting innovating WSMEs, including 478 getting access to preferential credit (Table 13).

Table 14 shows that only 2% of WSMEs participated in state training programs to strengthen human resources. Of these, about half received state support (e.g., lower fees). In recent years, the state has been promoting on-the-job and in-house training and demand-based training for SMEs, especially those in manufacturing. On-the-job and in-house training should be expanded nationwide, and there need to be better connections between state training and other vocational training or training firms in terms of course design and delivery. The training should include additional e-learning courses as part of blended training delivery, given that WSME owners and managers are usually busy. In addition, apart from traditional training, capacity building for WSMEs should consist of individual coaching to meet their specific needs.

Many more WSMEs (28%) reported undertaking one or more forms of digital transformation (Table 15), although less than half of these had any form of digital transformation plan. This was most common in medium-size WSMEs, but much more common in the north compared to the south. Digital transformation, however, was about the same across all sectors. Nearly 9,000 WSMEs were developing e-commerce or online business models. The most common forms of digital transformation related to corporate governance documents and new software.

Questionnaire 1.15 about WSMEs also collected data about those that had transformed from household businesses to become enterprises (Table 16), and about access to and demand for new loans and investors (Table 17). Only 3% of WSMEs reported having transformed from a household business. This suggests that the cost of being an enterprise generally outweighs the benefits of remaining a household business. The state supported 62% of the 2,863 who did transform, with procedural guidance and financial consulting being the most common types of support. Despite Decree No. 39/2018/ND-CP removing license fees for the first three years of business registration and providing free advice and guidance on tax administrative procedures, the conversion of household businesses to formal enterprises remains at a low level.[17] Manufacturing and trading WSMEs were more likely to make the transition from a household business.

---

[17]   Research Report of Facilitation Solutions for Production and Business Activities for Vietnamese Business Households (Báo cáo nghiên cứu giải pháp thuận lợi hoá hoạt động sản xuất, kinh doanh cho hộ kinh doanh Việt Nam). Vietnam Institute for Economics and Policy Research (VEPR) and BIDV Training and Research Institute. Ha Noi, 2021 (in Vietnamese)

Table 12: Five Types of State Support for Brand Development by Women-Owned Small and Medium-Sized Enterprises

Item	Number of WSMEs (Q 1.15)	Number of WSMEs Developing Brand Who Got at least One Type of State Support	Number of WSMEs by State Support Received in Brand Development						
			Total	Training in Knowledge and Skills on Building and Promoting Brand	Support for Brand naming; Design Logo or System of Brand Identifiers	Consulting Strategy to Build and Develop Brand	Support for Marketing Communication, and Promoting Brand	Supporting Enterprise to Protect Brand or Trademark Violation	Other
All WSMEs	**110,667**	**5,381**	**7,552**	**1,737**	**996**	**1,050**	**1,718**	**1,569**	**482**
By region									
Red River Delta	32,459	1,474	**2,086**	509	301	249	453	459	115
South East	47,238	1,730	**2,351**	508	337	325	521	460	200
Mekong River Delta	8,990	688	**1,003**	223	140	165	211	228	36
By size									
Medium	3,584	316	**492**	106	85	72	103	106	20
By sector									
Agriculture, forestry, and fishing	726	69	**103**	34	9	18	20	13	9
Mining and quarrying	289	14	**22**	7	3	3	3	5	1
Manufacturing	15,025	893	**1,317**	277	207	200	286	281	66
Electricity, gas, stream, and air conditioning supply	563	39	**52**	13	3	11	8	14	3
Water supply, sewerage, waste management, and remediation activities	341	10	**17**	4	1	2	2	7	1
Construction	7,441	340	**466**	135	45	75	89	76	46
Wholesale and retail trade; repair of motor vehicles and motorcycles	51,041	2,534	**3,492**	754	476	475	802	756	229

continued on next page

Table 12 continued

Item	Number of WSMEs (Q 1.15)	Number of WSMEs Developing Brand Who Got at least One Type of State Support	Number of WSMEs by State Support Received in Brand Development						
			Total	Training in Knowledge and Skills on Building and Promoting Brand	Support for Brand naming; Design Logo or System of Brand Identifiers	Consulting Strategy to Build and Develop Brand	Support for Marketing Communication, and Promoting Brand	Supporting Enterprise to Protect Brand or Trademark Violation	Other
Of which, wholesale and retail trade	48,921	2,419	3,317	715	456	450	753	726	217
Transportation and storage	7,045	227	326	76	34	51	83	63	19
Accommodation and food service activities	6,372	286	380	96	49	45	99	75	16
Information and communication	1,639	79	122	31	16	12	29	28	6
Financial, banking, and insurance activities	670	52	87	16	11	16	21	22	1
Real estate activities	2,425	111	145	31	21	15	38	27	13
Professional, scientific, and technical activities	7,422	315	443	95	56	60	105	84	43
Administrative and support service activities	5,134	215	307	81	33	35	82	60	16
Education and training	2,466	121	172	60	17	20	33	37	5
Human health and social work activities	557	33	51	18	10	8	8	4	3
Arts, entertainment, and recreation	567	15	19	4	3	2	3	6	1
Other service activities	944	28	31	5	2	2	7	11	4

WSMEs = women-owned small and medium-sized enterprises.
Source: General Statistics Office. 2021. Economic Census.

Table 13: Innovating Women-Owned Small and Medium-Sized Enterprises and Six Types of State Support

Item	Number of WSMEs (Q1.15)	Having Activities to Innovate, Improve Products, Services, Processes, and Business Models		WSMEs Implementing Innovation Activities Who Got at least One Type of State Support (Number)	WSMEs Implementing Innovation Activities Who Got at least One Type of State Support (%)	Number of WSMEs Implementing Innovation Activities by State Support Received							
		Number of WSMEs	% of All WSMEs			Total	Consulting on Intellectual Property, Exploitation, and Development of Intellectual Property	Support Procedures on Standards, Technical Regulations Perfecting New Products, New Business Models	Support for Technology Application and Transfer	Support for Training, Information, and Trade Promotion of Technology Products and Services	Support Using Technical Facilities, Incubators, and Co-working Areas	Supporting Preferential Credit Capital to Implement Innovation Activities	Other
All WSMEs	**110,667**	**13,040**	**12**	**2,511**	**19**	**3,620**	**619**	**868**	**514**	**908**	**185**	**478**	**48**
By region													
Red River Delta	32,459	4,477	14	729	16	1,043	209	242	150	261	50	118	13
South East	47,238	5,034	11	803	16	1,146	211	255	156	315	73	115	21
Mekong River Delta	8,990	1,039	12	367	35	533	79	146	96	115	16	80	1
By size													
Medium	3,584	949	26	187	20	292	57	80	40	70	10	35	0
By sector													
Agriculture, forestry, and fishing	726	102	14	44	43	78	13	20	13	12	14	6	0
Mining and quarrying	289	33	11	11	33	15	1	5	1	5	0	3	0
Manufacturing	15,025	2,926	19	553	19	872	136	232	154	179	56	102	13
Electricity, gas, stream, and air conditioning supply	563	57	10	19	33	21	2	7	5	3	0	3	1
Water supply, sewerage, waste management, and remediation activities	341	33	10	11	33	16	3	5	2	4	0	2	0

continued on next page

Table 13 continued

Item	Number of WSMEs (Q 1.15)	Having Activities to Innovate, Improve Products, Services, Processes, and Business Models		WSMEs Implementing Innovation Activities Who Got at least One Type of State Support (Number)	WSMEs Implementing Innovation Activities Who Got at least One Type of State Support (%)	Number of WSMEs Implementing Innovation Activities by State Support Received							
		Number of WSMEs	% of All WSMEs			Total	Consulting on Intellectual Property, Exploitation, and Development of Intellectual Property	Support Procedures on Standards, Technical Regulations Perfecting New Products, New Business Models	Support for Technology Application and Transfer	Support for Training, Information, and Trade Promotion of Technology Products and Services	Support Using Technical Facilities, Incubators, and Co-working Areas	Supporting Preferential Credit Capital to Implement Innovation Activities	Other
Construction	7,441	771	10	163	21	232	26	50	40	64	14	35	3
Wholesale and retail trade; repair of motor vehicles and motorcycles	51,041	5,357	10	1,039	19	1,424	241	361	164	361	54	225	18
Of which, wholesale and retail trade	48,921	5,124	10	992	19	1,363	232	348	157	343	51	214	18
Transportation and storage	7,045	577	8	105	18	153	17	32	28	49	7	18	2
Accommodation and food service activities	6,372	585	9	117	20	174	30	40	21	53	12	16	2
Information and communication	1,639	283	17	52	18	78	25	9	14	19	2	5	4
Financial, banking, and insurance activities	670	103	15	22	21	31	9	6	3	11	0	2	0
Real estate activities	2,425	194	8	38	20	49	14	13	2	15	1	4	0
Professional, scientific, and technical activities	7,422	840	11	136	16	189	41	41	28	51	7	19	2
Administrative and support service activities	5,134	548	11	89	16	131	31	15	19	41	8	16	1

continued on next page

Table 13 continued

Item	Number of WSMEs (Q 1.15)	Having Activities to Innovate, Improve Products, Services, Processes, and Business Models		WSMEs Implementing Innovation Activities Who Got at least One Type of State Support (Number)	WSMEs Implementing Innovation Activities Who Got at least One Type of State Support (%)	Number of WSMEs Implementing Innovation Activities by State Support Received							
		Number of WSMEs	% of All WSMEs			Total	Consulting on Intellectual Property, Exploitation, and Development of Intellectual Property	Support Procedures on Standards, Technical Regulations, Perfecting New Products, New Business Models	Support for Technology Application and Transfer	Support for Training, Information, and Trade Promotion of Technology Products and Services	Support Using Technical Facilities, Incubators, and Co-working Areas	Supporting Preferential Credit Capital to Implement Innovation Activities	Other
Education and training	2,466	400	16	74	19	98	19	16	12	30	5	15	1
Human health and social work activities	557	83	15	20	24	35	8	11	3	7	3	3	0
Arts, entertainment, and recreation	567	57	10	4	7	6	0	2	1	2	1	0	0
Other service activities	944	91	10	14	15	18	3	3	4	2	1	4	1

WSMEs = women-owned small and medium-sized enterprises.

Source: General Statistics Office. 2021. Economic Census.

Table 14: State-Delivered Human Resource Training for Women-Owned Small and Medium-Sized Enterprises

Item	Number of WSMEs (Q 1.15)	Participating in State-Delivered Training Programs to Improve Quality of Human Resources		WSMEs Participating in Training Programs to Improve Quality of Human Resources Who Got at least One Type of State Support (Number)	WSMEs Participating in Training Programs to Improve Quality of Human Resources Who Got at least One Type of State Support (%)	Number of WSMEs Participating in Training Programs to Improve Quality of Human Resources by State Support Received				
		Number of WSMEs	% of All WSMEs			Total	Exemption and Reduction of Costs for Training Courses on Business Start-up and Business Administration	Exemption and Reduction of Costs for Vocational Training Courses	Support for Direct Training in Enterprise	Other
All WSMEs	**110,667**	**2,271**	**2**	**1,157**	**51**	**1,374**	**489**	**396**	**428**	**61**
By region										
Red River Delta	32,459	780	2	350	45	409	155	119	111	24
South East	47,238	587	1	254	43	302	102	80	102	18
Mekong River Delta	8,990	218	2	160	73	204	65	71	66	2
By size										
Medium-size WSMEs	3,584	163	5	84	52	108	34	36	33	5
By sector										
Agriculture, forestry, and fishing	726	25	3	19	76	24	13	4	7	0
Mining and quarrying	289	8	3	4	50	6	2	1	3	0
Manufacturing	15,025	330	2	168	51	205	74	56	67	8
Electricity, gas, stream, and air conditioning supply	563	20	4	12	60	17	7	6	4	0

continued on next page

Table 14 continued

Item	Number of WSMEs (Q 1.15)	Participating in State-Delivered Training Programs to Improve Quality of Human Resources		WSMEs Participating in Training Programs to Improve Quality of Human Resources Who Got at least One Type of State Support (Number)	WSMEs Participating in Training Programs to Improve Quality of Human Resources Who Got at least One Type of State Support (%)	Number of WSMEs Participating in Training Programs to Improve Quality of Human Resources by State Support Received				
		Number of WSMEs	% of All WSMEs			Total	Exemption and Reduction of Costs for Training Courses on Business Start-up and Business Administration	Exemption and Reduction of Costs for Vocational Training Courses	Support for Direct Training in Enterprise	Other
Water supply, sewerage, waste management, and remediation activities	341	7	2	2	29	2	1	1	0	0
Construction	7,441	181	2	89	49	95	42	24	29	0
Wholesale and retail trade; repair of motor vehicles and motorcycles	51,041	880	2	443	50	525	186	147	169	23
Of which, wholesale and retail trade	48,921	833	2	419	50	495	175	140	159	21
Transportation and storage	7,045	126	2	58	46	67	23	16	25	3
Accommodation and food service activities	6,372	135	2	84	62	98	28	37	25	8
Information and communication	1,639	33	2	17	52	21	9	4	7	1
Financial, banking, and insurance activities	670	21	3	11	52	13	0	3	10	0
Real estate activities	2,425	52	2	27	52	31	16	10	5	0

continued on next page

Table 14 *continued*

Item	Number of WSMEs (Q 1.15)	Participating in State-Delivered Training Programs to Improve Quality of Human Resources		WSMEs Participating in Training Programs to Improve Quality of Human Resources Who Got at least One Type of State Support (Number)	WSMEs Participating in Training Programs to Improve Quality of Human Resources Who Got at least One Type of State Support (%)	Number of WSMEs Participating in Training Programs to Improve Quality of Human Resources by State Support Received				
		Number of WSMEs	% of All WSMEs			Total	Exemption and Reduction of Costs for Training Courses on Business Start-up and Business Administration	Exemption and Reduction of Costs for Vocational Training Courses	Support for Direct Training in Enterprise	Other
Professional, scientific, and technical activities	7,422	164	2	70	43	82	34	19	22	7
Administrative and support service activities	5,134	111	2	59	53	75	22	23	23	7
Education and training	2,466	120	5	67	56	79	21	33	23	2
Human health and social work activities	557	34	6	16	47	21	5	9	6	1
Arts, entertainment, and recreation	567	10	2	5	50	6	3	2	1	0
Other service activities	944	14	1	6	43	7	3	1	2	1

WSMEs = women-owned small and medium-sized enterprises.
Source: General Statistics Office. 2021. Economic Census.

Table 15: Digital Transformation of Women-Owned Small and Medium-Sized Enterprises

Item	Number of WSMEs (Q1.15)	Implementing Digital Transformation		Number of WSMEs by Forms of Digital Transformation					Having a Digital Transformation Plan in Future	
		Number of WSMEs	% of All WSMEs	Digitalization of Corporate Governance Documents	Digitalization of Management Process	Develop a Business Channel Online Business Model	Participate in e-Commerce	Using Software in Production and Business Activities	Number of WSMEs	% of All WSMEs
All WSMEs	**110,667**	**30,743**	**28**	**14,997**	**2,509**	**2,753**	**6,095**	**16,564**	**14,428**	**13**
By region										
Red River Delta	32,459	14,191	44	6,717	1,049	1,143	2,241	8,437	5,612	17
South East	47,238	8,947	19	4,296	784	952	2,231	4,365	4,906	10
Mekong River Delta	8,990	1,915	21	1,061	197	190	404	844	1,022	11
By size										
Medium-size WSMEs	3,584	1,610	45	774	196	142	358	1,009	749	21
By sector										
Agriculture, forestry, and fishing	726	154	21	80	20	17	36	78	81	11
Mining and quarrying	289	75	26	41	4	2	15	34	31	11
Manufacturing	15,025	3,966	26	2,090	431	324	891	2,020	2,149	14
Electricity, gas, stream, and air conditioning supply	563	152	27	76	13	14	19	80	78	14
Water supply, sewerage, waste management, and remediation activities	341	72	21	37	10	2	6	39	38	11
Construction	7,441	2,013	27	1,021	157	87	293	1,104	903	12
Wholesale and retail trade; repair of motor vehicles and motorcycles	51,041	14,489	28	6,867	1,003	1,318	3,179	7,809	6,586	13

continued on next page

Table 15 continued

Item	Number of WSMEs (Q 1.15)	Implementing Digital Transformation		Number of WSMEs by Forms of Digital Transformation					Having a Digital Transformation Plan in Future	
		Number of WSMEs	% of All WSMEs	Digitalization of Corporate Governance Documents	Digitalization of Management Process	Develop a Business Channel Online Business Model	Participate in e-Commerce	Using Software in Production and Business Activities	Number of WSMEs	% of All WSMEs
Of which, wholesale and retail trade	48,921	13,895	28	6,569	962	1,260	3,060	7,471	6,308	13
Transportation and storage	7,045	1,811	26	879	129	136	283	1,020	817	12
Accommodation and food service activities	6,372	1,479	23	723	144	150	289	789	642	10
Information and communication	1,639	649	40	315	77	83	142	384	331	20
Financial, banking, and insurance activities	670	209	31	110	22	46	35	101	96	14
Real estate activities	2,425	683	28	323	54	51	97	380	298	12
Professional, scientific, and technical activities	7,422	2,249	30	1,094	184	198	339	1,249	1,095	15
Administrative and support service activities	5,134	1,462	28	718	112	163	269	780	665	13
Education and training	2,466	723	29	359	94	97	102	388	352	14
Human health and social work activities	557	232	42	108	35	24	35	148	111	20
Arts, entertainment, and recreation	567	133	23	63	8	15	26	71	64	11
Other service activities	944	192	20	93	12	26	39	90	91	10

WSMEs = women–owned small and medium–sized enterprises.

Source: GSO. 2021. Economic Census.

Table 16: Women-Owned Small and Medium-Sized Enterprises Graduated from Household Businesses

Item	Number of WSMEs (Q 1.15)	Transforming from Household Business		WSMEs Transforming from Household Business Who Got at least One Type of State Support (Number)	WSMEs Transforming from Household Business Who Got at least One Type of State Support (%)	Number of WSMEs Transforming from Household Business by State Support Received						
		Number of WSMEs	% of All WSMEs			Total	Consulting, Guiding Documents and Procedures for Setting up an Enterprise	No fees for First Time Business Registration or Announcements	No Fees for First Business License for Conditional Business Lines	Free of License Tax for Three Years from Date of First Registration Certificate	Consulting, Guiding Tax Administrative Procedures and Accounting Regime	Other
All WSMEs	**110,667**	**2,863**	**3**	**1,764**	**62**	**3,349**	**1,486**	**409**	**164**	**332**	**947**	**11**
By region												
Red River Delta	32,459	723	2	397	55	**694**	323	60	16	56	239	0
South East	47,238	500	1	248	50	**411**	202	54	12	30	112	1
Mekong River Delta	8,990	496	6	362	73	**740**	299	95	43	104	195	4
By size												
Medium–size WSMEs	3,584	55	2	35	64	**62**	24	8	3	8	19	0
By sector												
Agriculture, forestry, and fishing	726	36	5	24	67	**37**	18	9	1	5	4	0
Mining and quarrying	289	10	3	4	40	**7**	4	1	0	1	1	0
Manufacturing	15,025	398	3	237	60	**454**	198	61	23	55	117	0
Electricity, gas, stream, and air conditioning supply	563	12	2	9	75	**19**	8	4	0	1	6	0
Water supply, sewerage, waste management, and remediation activities	341	14	4	8	57	**12**	7	1	1	1	2	0
Construction	7,441	89	1	67	75	**129**	60	19	5	13	31	1
Wholesale and retail trade; repair of motor vehicles and motorcycles	51,041	1,831	4	1,132	62	**2,140**	952	247	98	203	631	9

continued on next page

Table 16 continued

Item	Number of WSMEs (Q 1.15)	Transforming from Household Business		WSMEs Transforming from Household Business Who Got at least One Type of State Support (Number)	WSMEs Transforming from Household Business Who Got at least One Type of State Support (%)	Number of WSMEs Transforming from Household Business by State Support Received						
		Number of WSMEs	% of All WSMEs			Total	Consulting, Guiding Documents and Procedures for Setting up an Enterprise	No fees for First Time Business Registration or Announcements	No Fees for First Business License for Conditional Business Lines	Free of License Tax for Three Years from Date of First Registration Certificate	Consulting, Guiding Tax Administrative Procedures and Accounting Regime	Other
Of which, wholesale and retail trade	48,921	1,764	4	1,095	62	2,071	926	240	94	193	610	8
Transportation and storage	7,045	91	1	55	60	110	44	14	4	10	38	0
Accommodation and food service activities	6,372	192	3	121	63	236	104	26	18	23	65	0
Information and communication	1,639	9	1	4	44	7	4	1	0	1	1	0
Financial, banking, and insurance activities	670	10	1	6	60	13	5	2	2	0	4	0
Real estate activities	2,425	23	1	15	65	19	11	0	0	1	7	0
Professional, scientific, and technical activities	7,422	46	1	27	59	49	22	9	2	2	14	0
Administrative and support service activities	5,134	31	1	16	52	35	15	5	4	4	7	0
Education and training	2,466	26	1	17	65	36	16	5	2	5	8	0
Human health and social work activities	557	14	3	9	64	20	7	1	1	3	7	1
Arts, entertainment, and recreation	567	8	1	5	63	7	4	1	0	1	1	0
Other service activities	944	23	2	8	35	19	7	3	3	3	3	0

WSMEs = women-owned small and medium-sized enterprises.
Source: GSO. 2021. Economic Census.

A crucial difference between being a household business and being an enterprise is that the latter is incorporated, which allows then access to financing as a company. Table 17 shows that 20% of all WSMEs had outstanding loans at the time of the survey. WSMEs with loans were more frequent in the north than in the south, and 52% of medium-size WSMEs had loans. The first four sectors listed in Table 17 had high rates of loans. Access to preferential credit was only obtained by 6% of WSMEs and 20% of medium-size WSMEs.

Demand for ongoing credit was reported by 26% of WSMEs, particularly those in the construction and manufacturing sectors. Demand for investment capital was reported by 20% of WSMEs but only 35% of medium-size WSMEs. Loans and demand for capital were stronger in the north than in the south. Investment capital was sought across all sectors.

Tables 6 to 17 with data from Questionnaire 1.15 have provided further insights into the numbers and nature of dynamic WSMEs in Viet Nam. The dynamic indicators seem healthy for WSMEs: 28% are undertaking digital transformations, 12% doing innovations, 22% have websites, and 10% have product or service certifications. The data also shows differences between regions and sectors and that the state has supported these dynamic WSMEs to a significant extent. Probably over 50% of dynamic WSMEs have benefited from at least one type of state support.

The financial data (Table 17) raises questions about the causes for differences in data. Demand for loans "in the future" (26%) is only slightly higher than those presently having loans (20%) and only slightly higher than those with demand for investment capital (20%). This data is corroborated by a report survey from Component 1 of the WAVES program, Technical Assistance 9660 (Regional): Promoting Transformative Gender Equality Agenda in Asia and the Pacific reported that 14% of women-led companies "are financially unserved."[18] That survey also reported from bank data that only 2% of WSME loans were in arrears, compared to 3% for all SMEs.

The data indicate a need for financial institutions and the state to adopt more innovative and targeted approaches to meet the financial needs of dynamic WSMEs.

---

[18]   This Component 1 report title is Financial Access of Women-Owned Small and Medium-Sized Enterprises in Viet Nam (ADB, December 2022). This report was also an important input to this White Book.

Table 17: Women-Owned Small and Medium-Sized Enterprises Use and Demand for Finance

Item	Number of WSMEs (Q 1.15)	Having Loans for Production and Business Activities		Having Access to Preferential Credit		Having Demand for Loan from Credit Institutions to Serve Production and Business activities in the future		Having Demand for Seeking Investment Capital Resources from Investors to Serve Production and Business Activities in Coming Time
		Number of WSMEs	% of All WSMEs	Number of WSMEs	% of All WSMEs	Number of WSMEs	% of All WSMEs	% of All WSMEs
All WSMEs	**110,667**	**21,733**	**20**	**6,532**	**6**	**29,196**	**26**	**20**
By region								
Red River Delta	32,459	7,206	22	1,858	6	9,410	29	24
South East	47,238	6,541	14	1,652	3	9,239	20	14
Mekong River Delta	8,990	1,897	21	780	9	2,919	32	22
By size								
Medium-size WSMEs	3,584	1,873	52	717	20	1,957	55	35
By sector								
Agriculture, forestry, and fishing	726	230	32	78	11	311	43	30
Mining and quarrying	289	98	34	35	12	109	38	25
Manufacturing	15,025	3,472	23	1,091	7	4,560	30	23
Electricity, gas, stream, and air conditioning supply	563	233	41	87	15	214	38	28
Water supply, sewerage, waste management, and remediation activities	341	61	18	26	8	82	24	17
Construction	7,441	1,822	24	600	8	2,684	36	27
Wholesale and retail trade; repair of motor vehicles and motorcycles	51,041	11,099	22	3,324	7	14,371	28	20

continued on next page

Table 17 continued

Item	Number of WSMEs (Q 1.15)	Having Loans for Production and Business Activities		Having Access to Preferential Credit		Having Demand for Loan from Credit Institutions to Serve Production and Business activities in the future		Having Demand for Seeking Investment Capital Resources from Investors to Serve Production and Business Activities in Coming Time
		Number of WSMEs	% of All WSMEs	Number of WSMEs	% of All WSMEs	Number of WSMEs	% of All WSMEs	% of All WSMEs
Of which, wholesale and retail trade	48,921	10,539	22	3,143	6	13,706	28	20
Transportation and storage	7,045	1,621	23	477	7	1,916	27	19
Accommodation and food service activities	6,372	796	12	225	4	1,188	19	15
Information and communication	1,639	150	9	30	2	246	15	17
Financial, banking, and insurance activities	670	79	12	26	4	129	19	18
Real estate activities	2,425	424	17	117	5	533	22	19
Professional, scientific, and technical activities	7,422	645	9	153	2	1,158	16	15
Administrative and support service activities	5,134	563	11	139	3	948	18	17
Education and training	2,466	225	9	67	3	377	15	16
Human health and social work activities	557	75	13	26	5	109	20	18
Arts, entertainment, and recreation	567	54	10	13	2	108	19	18
Other service activities	944	86	9	18	2	153	16	14

WSMEs = women-owned small and medium-sized enterprises.

Source: General Statistics Office. 2021. Economic Census.

4

Barriers Facing Women-Owned Small and Medium-Sized Enterprises

This chapter sets out the most significant barriers to the growth and development of WSMEs in Viet Nam. This information is drawn from interviews conducted with a small number of WSMEs.[19] While data collected about their perceptions of various forms of gender bias is largely opinion-based and highly qualitative, the results, where relevant, align with and sometimes explain the data reported in the GSO 2021 Economic Census. As such, this modest survey is a valuable supplement to the GSO data because it provides insights into biases and reasons for barriers to business faced by women. However, care should be taken in drawing conclusions due to biases in self-reporting of perceptions and the small sample size.

Resource-Based Barriers

This first category outlines barriers women entrepreneurs face in terms of access to resources. These are practical and observable impediments to growth and development.

Limited Access to Finance and Credit Support

WSMEs self-identified limited access to finance as a major barrier to the growth of their businesses. The respondents noted that these difficulties were not necessarily due to discriminatory practices on the part of banks and other financial lenders. For instance, when asked whether it matters if it is a man or a woman business owner applying for a bank loan, 89% of respondents either agreed or strongly agreed that being a man or a woman "made no difference" (Figure 3). According to the 2021 Economic Census data, WSMEs' share of total loan financing is about the same as their share of SME ownership (20%), and 68% of both men-owned SMEs and WSMEs reported having one or more loans requiring interest payments. There is scope for supporting experiments to expand bank lending instruments and for targeting WSMEs as a segmented market for higher lending (and profit).

Relying solely on self-reported responses cannot provide a conclusive answer to whether there is discrimination in banking practices. To accurately address this question, a thorough assessment of all factors that affect credit allocation must be

---

[19] One hundred eighteen WSME owners participated in the survey (n=118).

conducted. That percentage of the finance gap that cannot be explained by other factors such as business sector, risk factors associated with business conditions, and maturity need to be identified through rigorous evaluation.

Furthermore, lenders cannot evade their obligations, given that the provision of a uniform banking framework for all customers which fails to consider the unique requirements of WSMEs runs counter to the objective of facilitating WSMEs' access to finance. Thus, it may be necessary to customize regulations to accommodate the distinctive financial circumstances and business characteristics of women entrepreneurs to enhance their accessibility to financial resources.

Figure 3: Rate of Perceived Differences between Treatment of Men versus Women Applying for Bank Loans

Agree or Disagree: *"Banks follow strict guidelines and criteria to give loans to businesses, so it does not matter that it is a man or a woman business owner applying for the loan."*

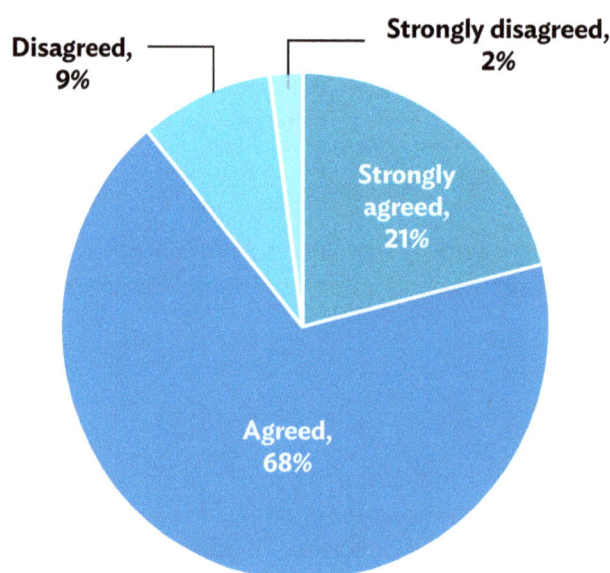

Source: Palladium-Mekong Economics. 2022. WSME Survey (n=118).

When targeted financial support is available, however, the uptake from WSMEs is often lower than expected, largely due to uncertainty, complicated procedures, low awareness, and self-selection bias. For example, in Thua Thien Hue Province, both the Small and Medium-Sized Enterprise Development Fund (SMEDF) and the Investment and Development Fund (IDF) offer preferential loans for SMEs, typically with interest rates 5%–6% lower than at commercial banks. Yet, few WSMEs have received SMEDF or IDF funding. WSMEs in the province believe this is due to limited understanding of the funding process and a common perception that applications will likely be rejected. Barriers to entry to obtain a share of such subsidized credit are perceived, rightly or wrongly, as too difficult for most WSMEs. Typically, on the demand side, such barriers have included a perceived lack of collateral, inadequate financial infrastructure, or the high cost of funding as well as nonfinancial barriers including social and cultural norms underlying gender biases, as well as the tendency for women-owned SMEs to be smaller and have limited access to business education opportunities and networks. Furthermore, access to limited allotments of cheap loans requires business networks that are male-dominated SMEs, unless there are WSME-only quotas. Supply-side barriers include the lack of gender-specific response strategies and a lack of gender-disaggregated data.[20]

In Lam Dong Province, women-led start-ups can also access financing that is typically 2.5–5 times greater than loan amounts available from commercial banks. This is a program run through the Women's Support Fund (WSF), managed in partnership with the Provincial Women's Union. However, WSMEs again cite a lack of understanding on how to apply for WSF funding.

Additionally, while there are many regulations that try to support credit acquisition for WSMEs, they are still unable to acquire the credit they need.[21] Although this analysis cannot be directly compared with men-owned SMEs and while the government has provided credit incentives for SMEs, these are primarily allocated to priority sectors and not to WSMEs in particular. The SME Support Law specifies principles of prioritizing support to SMEs to access credit but does not have specific regulations to support the credit access of WSMEs and SMEs in general

Limited Supply of Information Related to Small and Medium-Sized Enterprise Development Support

WSME Survey respondents identified limited access to information on business development support as the most significant barrier they faced, after household management burdens. This issue was also identified during stakeholder discussions with local government agencies in each of the four provinces.

---

[20] Iinternational Finance Corporation. 2017. Women-Owned Enterprises in Vietnam: Perceptions and Potential.
[21] Including laws (e.g., Law 04/2017/QH14 and Law 73/2006/QH11), Government Decrees (e.g., Decree No. 80/2021/ND-CP and Decree No. 34/2018/ND-CP), Prime Minister's Decisions (e.g., Decision No. 149/2020/QD-TTg and Decision No. 2351/2021/QD-TTg), SBV circulars (e.g., Circular No. 45/2018/TT-NHNN, Circular No. 39/2016/TT-NHNN, Circular No. 41/2016/TT-NHNN, Circular 05/2020//TT-NHNN and Circular No. 10/2021/TT-NHNN), policies, and programs for SMEs, including WSMEs, focusing on supporting enterprises to access credit through preferential measures such as credit guarantees, interest rate ceilings, or management support. There are a couple of main mechanisms used to promote the development of and access to finance for SMEs. However, the number of programs specifically targeting WSMEs is quite limited. It should be noted that these programs are mostly unfunded and hence carry little incentive for commercial banks, which have full discretion in implementing these measures. The first mechanism is easier access to loans from credit institutions. SBV has directed credit institutions to simplify loan procedures for SMEs for production and business purposes (SBV Directive No. 6627/NHNN-TD dated 4 September 2018). The Banking Business Connection Program was created in 2014 to provide a forum in which banks and businesses can discuss experiences and challenges related to accessing bank loans and try to find workable solutions. The second mechanism is through flexible collateral requirements. The Government sets preferential collateral requirements for SMEs operating in priority productive sectors and in rural areas (Government Decree No. 55/2015/ND-CP and Decree No. 116/2018/ND-CP). As SMEs' ability to negotiate with banks on collateral is limited, some SBV policies encourage banks to provide trust collateral. The third mechanism is access to preferential borrowing rates. For example, as per SBV Circular No. 39/2016/TT-NHNN, SMEs are of five priority groups to be eligible to borrow within the regulatory cap on Viet Nam Dong short term lending interest rates. Government Decree No. 31/2022/ND-CP, for 2% interest subsidies provided in the state budget for loans to certain groups of enterprises, cooperatives, and household businesses during 2022–2023. The last mechanism is the use of specific products and services for WSMEs. For instance, a 2016 joint program among SBV, the Viet Nam Women's Union, the Viet Nam Farmers' Union, and credit institutions have created a cooperation framework to implement programs aimed at supporting access to capital and financial skills for Viet Nam Women's Union members.

In broad terms, WSMEs explained they have limited information on support mechanisms and general business development procedures. This affects both long-term business planning and day-to-day management. For example, a WSME may wish to apply for a loan, join a business network, or formally register their enterprise, but do not know how or where to start this process. Several respondents also spoke of a lack of guidance on tax and financial matters such as when to submit a tax report, resulting in penalties for delayed submission. This limited access to SME Development Support is somewhat reflected in the percentage of WSMEs' receiving state support when transforming from household businesses as reported by GSO 2021 Economic Census. According to the GSO census, of 2,863 surveyed WSMEs, who converted from household businesses, only 52% received guidance to transition to an enterprise with 33% receiving state support relating to tax procedures; notably, 38% said they did not receive any state support of any sort (Table 16).

The same can be said of existing training and mentoring schemes. WSMEs reported that they often heard about support programs but received little formal information on how to apply or struggled with complicated administrative procedures and eligibility requirements. This might be one of the causes leading to the very low rate of WSME participation in training sessions provided by the government to improve the quality of human resources. As reported in the 2021 Economic Census, as little as 2% of the 110,667 WSMEs surveyed partook in these state-delivered training programs (Table 14).

Respondents stated that government agencies often do not provide disseminate clear and accessible information about available SME support policies on television or social media channels or through business associations etc.,. for easily accessible specifically for women entrepreneurs. For example, in Lam Dong Province, WSME respondents were not aware of existing initiatives offering digital marketing training to business leaders. It may be because of lack of state budget for government agencies to disseminate the information. Moreover, commercial banks do not publish standardized information about financial products or interest rates.[22]

Limited Managerial, Marketing, and Business Administration Skills

WSMEs and other stakeholders also identified poor managerial, marketing, and business administration skills as a barrier to business development. Moreover, they highlighted a lack of training and capacity building opportunities specifically for women entrepreneurs seeking to improve their management skills.

In discussions with the Viet Nam Women's Union in Thua Thien Hue Province, respondents explained there is a training and capacity building gap for union members on several aspects of business management, training programs for business start-up support, programs to support household businesses to convert to formally established enterprises, incubation programs and accelerator platforms, support for product development, and mentoring schemes for business-to-business (B2B) joint activities and collaboration. To illustrate, the 2021 Economic

---

[22]   International Monetary Fund database (accessed September 2022). https://data.imf.org/regular.
aspx?key=61545855.

Census reports that 41% of women-owned household-business graduates surveyed in Thua Thien Hue did not receive any state support, in comparison with the regional average of 29%. Notably, none of the WSMEs surveyed received any government-supported technical facilities and incubators when implementing innovation activities (Appendix 3, Table A3.2).

In Lam Dong Province, the Young Entrepreneurs Association highlighted similar ideas, emphasizing the lack of a start-up ecosystem for WSMEs.

Several respondents across the four provinces also called attention to how limited managerial and business administration skills lead to difficulties in training and developing staff within their enterprise. In many cases, women owners lack the resources to train and improve skills for middle-level managers, which contributes to low productivity and high staff turnover. This also aligns with the findings in the 2020 UN Women's study on WSMEs, i.e., they have disadvantages when it comes to human and social capital, and therefore a lack of knowledge and skills and access to qualified labor remains a barrier.[23]

Lack of Access to Technology

WSMEs identified a lack of access to technology as another barrier to their growth. This is despite that during COVID-19, many enterprises had to quickly adapt to digital business models, particularly in the fields of marketing and sales, by developing commercial websites. This was a difficult transition for many SMEs as they have little digital knowledge and technical support. The 2021 Economic Census data shows that of 13,040 WSMEs surveyed with innovative activities, many of which have technical aspects to them, 81% did not receive any state support (Table 13).

In Lam Dong Province, WSMEs identified a need for guidance to help them choose the right digital marketing approach (e.g., how to invest efficiently in online marketing platforms to grow their respective businesses).

Limited Knowledge of Accounting Procedures and Best Practice

Results from the WSME survey indicated that limited accounting skills are another barrier to growth. Women owners self-report receiving little to no training in cash flow management, strategy planning, or balance sheet administration. Limited accounting knowledge was also reported by lenders. For example, the IDF claimed that it can be time-consuming to assess loan applications from WSMEs because the accounts are often poorly prepared, with key financial information missing or unclear. "Account personnel of WSMEs are friendly and nice to work with, but they are not equipped with professional skills in investment project management," said an IDF spokesperson.

---

[23] UN Women. 2020. *A Review of the Implementation of SMEs Support Legislation and the Capacity Building Needs and Training Services for WSMEs and Women Entrepreneurs in Viet Nam.* https://vietnam.un.org/en/109986-review-implementation-small-and-medium-enterprises-smes-support-legislation-and-capacity.

Legal and Regulatory Framework

In general, WSMEs did not identify the application of the legal and policy framework as a particularly important barrier relative to men-owned SMEs. For instance, when asked about the statement in Figure 4, 86% of respondents did not think that WSMEs encounter more regulatory challenges than men-owned businesses. Concerning implementation, however, while 69% for those who disagree, and 31% who agree (Figure 5).

Figure 4: Rate of Perceived Differences between Men versus Women Business Owners in Terms of Legal and Regulatory Compliance

Agree or Disagree: "Female business owners in Viet Nam encounter more challenges or barriers in terms of legal and regulatory compliance compared with male business owners."

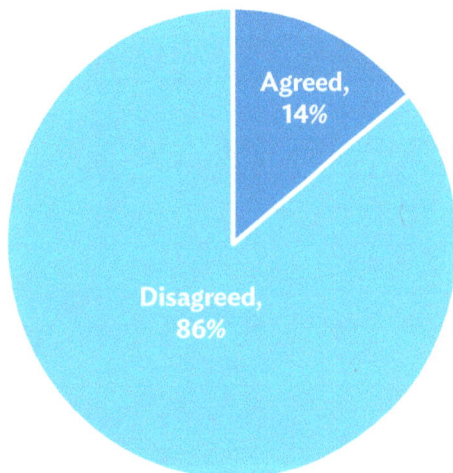

Agreed, 14%

Disagreed, 86%

Source: Palladium-Mekong Economics. 2022. WSME Survey (n=118).

Figure 5: Rate of Perceived Differences between Treatment of Men versus Women Business Owners by Government Officials

Agree or Disagree: "Government officials, both male and female, treat men doing business more favorable than they do with women in business."

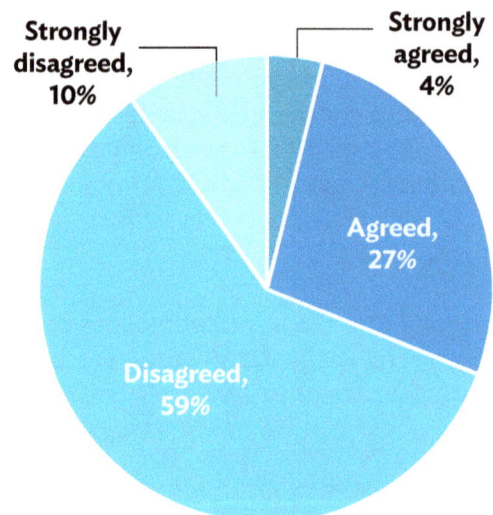

Strongly disagreed, 10%

Strongly agreed, 4%

Agreed, 27%

Disagreed, 59%

Source: Palladium-Mekong Economics. 2022. WSME Survey (n=118).

Figure 6: Perceptions of Men-Dominated Business Networks by Women Business Owners

Agree or Disagree: "Women are good networkers, but men have a monopoly on (control of) many formal and social networks for doing business."

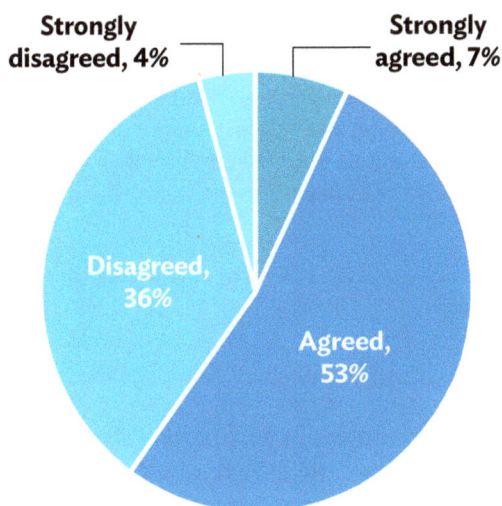

Strongly disagreed, 4%

Strongly agreed, 7%

Disagreed, 36%

Agreed, 53%

Source: Palladium-Mekong Economics. 2022. WSME Survey (n=118).

Social Barriers

The following section examines the social barriers to women's entrepreneurship, focusing on the role of gender-based norms and self-selection in the business landscape.

Social barriers for women entrepreneurs start from birth in the form of gendered social norms and customary expectations. As children and young adults, girls and boys are treated differently. The girls are taught to be gentle, quiet, and defer to others, to be followers, to make sacrifices, and to show empathy. Not all fit that mold, but the pressure to conform is strong. Conversely, boys are encouraged to be more ambitious and demanding. These are the social norms and values that build expectations about how girls should behave and think (Box 1).

These social norms become a decades-long tax on the time and energy of women compared to men. In such an environment, women can find themselves choosing not to start or grow a business (i.e., engaging in self-selection), while also facing discrimination when they do try to start a business.

Box 1: Gendered Legacy of Confucianism in Vietnamese Society

Over the past two decades, a body of literature has examined the legacy of Confucianism to explain the prevalence of distinct gender roles within Vietnamese social culture and tradition.

Confucianism can be broadly considered a system of ethics that revolves around moral values that stress harmonious interpersonal relations. For women, filial piety is a main tenet of Confucian thought. This refers to a general attitude of obedience and devotion to one's seniors as the basis of individual moral conduct and social harmony. Women are held responsible for the well-being of the family and taught to put the family's interests ahead of their own. Typically, this duty manifests through the act of being a subordinate wife and mother. Traits such as being generally compliant, silent, and modest are required. Mirroring this, men are looked down on should they choose to undertake duties deemed beneath them such as cooking or childcare; their role is confined to being the breadwinner of the family.[a]

---

[a]   Mai Trang Vu and Thi Thanh Thuy Pham. 2021. Still in the Shadow of Confucianism? Gender Bias in Contemporary English Textbooks in Viet Nam, Pedagogy, Culture and Society. DOI: 10.1080/14681366.2021.19242392021.

In this context, self-selection refers to a situation whereby a woman decides not to try starting a business or limits the growth of an existing one.[24] This happens because of barriers in terms of access to resources and the social expectation that women should not be as business-minded or ambitious as men. Some women might start a business but settle for a modest income that gives them time off for their household responsibilities.[25] Men, however, typically without such responsibilities, can dedicate more time to their business, take risks, and plan for growth. In other words, women face more social pressure to balance income-earning with domestic and care work.

Functional Household Burdens

Of the women business owners and women-focused professional and social organizations and business support organization surveyed, 79% identified household responsibilities as a major barrier to the growth of their business (Figure 7).[26]

Compared to men, women are expected to spend a significantly greater portion of their time on household responsibilities, placing their businesses at a severe disadvantage compared to men-owned enterprises. For example, ILO (2021) found that women, on average, spent 20 hours per week cleaning the house, washing clothes, cooking, shopping for the family, and childcare compared to 11 hours spent by men on the same duties. The research also found that one-fifth of men did not spend any time on these activities.[27]

---

[24]   Roth, Alvin E., and John H. Kagel. 2016. *The Handbook of Experimental Economics, Volume 2.* Princeton: Princeton University Press. muse.jhu.edu/book/64572. pp. 481–553.

[25]   Note: Another concern for some couples, and a constraint on women starting businesses and careers, is a degree of male jealousy if the wife earns considerably more income than the husband. This thinking may be old-fashioned and in decline, but it is still quite common. See, for example, Syrda J. 2020. Spousal Relative Income and Male Psychological Distress. *Personality and Social Psychology Bulletin.* 46(6): pp. 976–992.

[26]   Palladium-Mekong Economics. 2022. WSME Survey.

[27]   International Labour Organization. 2021. *COVID-19 Widens Existing Gender Inequalities, Creates New Gaps in Viet Nam.* https://www.ilo.org/hanoi/Informationresources/Publicinformation/Pressreleases/WCMS_774498/lang--en/index.htm.

Figure 7: Household Burden Experienced by Women in Business

Agree or Disagree: "Female business owners are disadvantaged because women are forced to spend more time than men on household tasks and taking care of children and/or relatives."

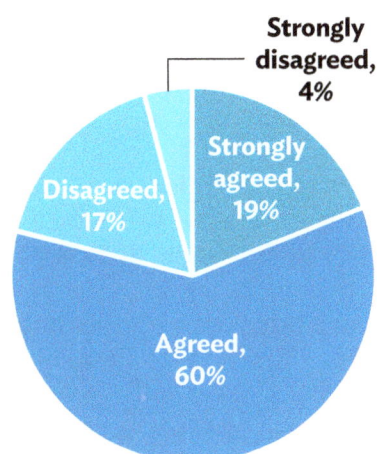

Strongly disagreed, 4%

Strongly agreed, 19%

Disagreed, 17%

Agreed, 60%

Source: Palladium-Mekong Economics. 2022. WSME Survey (n=118).

This disparity affects women regardless of their self-perception and ambition, with even the most motivated and aspiring women entrepreneurs still restricted. In simple terms, the typical male business owner has more time to work and grow his business compared to the typical woman business owner. This imbalance makes functional household burdens a significant barrier to acknowledge and address for more inclusive women's entrepreneurship. The issue is compounded by a lack of alternatives for women entrepreneurs, with limited access to affordable, accessible, and quality childcare options such as daycare centers and kindergartens.

Male-Dominated Business Networks

WSMEs identified male-dominated business networks as a barrier to growth (Figure 14). In Viet Nam, as in all countries, informal and formal business networks are crucial for business growth. Personal relationships with suppliers, similar businesses, government officials, investors, lawyers, and accountants are valuable business channels that facilitate entrepreneurship.

The problem for ambitious WSMEs is that these informal networks tend to be male-dominated, with few entry points for women entrepreneurs. Consequently, WSMEs miss out while men-owned businesses enjoy the benefits of greater information sharing and business referrals. For example, WSMEs described how men-owned businesses were better at overcoming legal constraints by "sliding through the back door," and having meals, drinking parties, or golf games with important stakeholders where they were able to gain a business advantage. As a result, it is harder for women entrepreneurs to engage with these business networks, and they are more likely to miss out on business opportunities.

Gender-Based Violence

Gender-based violence (GBV) is a specific barrier for WSMEs. A report by UN Women from 2010 reports several types of GBV in Viet Nam, including physical, sexual, and emotional violence.[28] There are several reports worldwide that show the relationship between GBV and low entrepreneurship numbers among women. Women who experience domestic violence face an increased fear of failure and sense of inadequacy, leading them to be less likely to initiate a new venture and become an entrepreneur.[29]

More common, however, is gender-based abuse and jealousy. Husbands, for example, sometimes resent wives who have grown a business and earn more than them. This can cause tensions and create pressures to allocate time back to household duties and the husband's needs. It also discourages women from focusing on their business. This may be a contributing factor to why the GSO data shows that only 3% of WSMEs are medium in size (and 69% are micro), compared to 5% of men-owned SMEs (64% are micro). While the amended Labor Code, which took effect in January 2021, aligns the law with Viet Nam's international obligations toward gender equality and addresses emergent issues around gender discrimination and sexual harassment in the workplace, real practice lags the legal framework. Much of the ongoing discrimination against Vietnamese businesswomen is driven by conscious and unconscious biases. An approach to supporting women in business must therefore understand these biases, measure them, and take actions to reduce them. Gender equality in business is enshrined in the law, but gender inequality is still perpetuated in gendered thinking and social norms around women's abilities, capacities, and commitments.

COVID-19 Impacts

This section discusses the challenges WSMEs faced because of the COVID-19 pandemic when compared to men-owned SMEs.

The COVID-19 pandemic put enormous pressure on businesses over the past two years as growth figures tumbled and most countries experienced recession. While Viet Nam's economy proved relatively resilient, being one of the few countries to post positive growth figures for 2020, its businesses were still hit hard, particularly those in the travel, tourism, and textile sectors, which in combination comprise the largest percentage of WSMEs.[30]

During 2020–2021, WSMEs consulted in this study, in general, reported impacts similar to those experienced by men-owned businesses. Those impacts include disruptions to their business operations, reduced consumer demand, staffing issues, supply chain disruptions, and higher costs and transit times for shipping

[28]   Sach BAO LUC GIOI CHUAN24.11.indd (unwomen.org) UNwomen 2010 (in Vietnamese).

[29]   Shahriar, A.Z. 2018. *Domestic Violence Prevents Women Realising Their Business Dreams.* https://impact. monash.edu/banking/domestic-violence-prevents-women-realising-their-business-dreams/.

[30]   UNwomen. 2020. *COVID-19 Socio-Economic Impact on Vulnerable Households and Enterprises.* https://www.undp.org/vietnam/publications/covid-19-socio-economic-impact-vulnerable-households-and-enterprises-gender-sensitive-assessment.

and domestic transport. These factors forced many businesses to either close or temporarily shut down as revenues dried up and business costs became insurmountable. Some 65%–69% of both WSMEs and men-owned SMEs reported lower revenues in 2020 compared to 2019. Sixty-nine percent of women-owned businesses reported that their 2021 estimate of revenues were lower than in 2020.[31] Worker layoffs in 2020 were reported by about 90% of both WSMEs and men-owned SMEs.

> *Revenue reductions were severe; 92% decrease in 2020 compared to 2019, and an expected 99% decrease in 2021. We've been experiencing losses for two years, with no financial resources to cover our fixed expenses.*
>
> — Do Thi Minh Tam, Director of Thanh Tam Tourist Services

During interviews, women SME owners identified several mechanisms through which COVID-19 had gendered impacts. First, as schools closed and children switched to remote learning, a greater burden was placed on women as childcare providers. UN Women reported that the number of Vietnamese women spending three or more hours doing non-paid domestic work increased by 73% in 2020.[32] Women were also more likely to venture out from the home to purchase food and other household commodities, putting themselves at greater risk of infection.

> *When the pandemic occurred, I could see that most women had to do more childcare and household chores than men.*
>
> — Son Loi, Mother, Vinh Phuc Province

With lockdowns and curfew restrictions in place, the ability of a business to transfer online through social media, websites, and mobile applications became paramount. WSMEs, who on average ran smaller SMEs in trade and other service areas, had less capacity to go online and gained fewer benefits. The pandemic made this barrier more acutely felt, leaving WSMEs at a greater disadvantage compared to men-owned businesses. The sharp decline in household incomes often led to women allocating more time to household duties rather than their businesses or careers and impacted mental well-being.[33]

COVID-19 impacts also varied by sector. Women-owned businesses saw a larger fall in revenue in the agriculture processing and tourism sectors compared to men-owned firms in the same industry, yet businesses in the manufacturing sector incurred a smaller reduction in revenue by the same comparison. In the agriculture processing sector, women-owned businesses achieved average 2020 revenues of only 27% compared to 2019 (men-owned SMES 42%).

---

[31] VCCI-USAID. Provincial Competitiveness Index (PCI) Survey 2021.

[32] UN Women. 2020. *Guidance Note for Action: Supporting SMEs to Ensure the COVID-19 Economic Recovery is Gender Responsive and Inclusive.* https://asiapacific.unwomen.org/sites/default/files/Field%20Office%20 ESEAsia/Docs/Publications/2020/04/SMEs-f.pdf.

[33] CARE. 2020. *CARE Rapid Gender Analysis for COVID-19 Viet Nam.*

A total of 95% of WSME owners interviewed in a ADB report, who had raised capital in the 12 months in 2021, had borrowed from a commercial bank.[34] Only about 7% had borrowed from money lenders or individual lenders, and an even smaller percentage from microfinance institutions, peer-to-peer platforms, or cooperatives and credit funds. The share of WSMEs that had borrowed from family and friends over the previous 12 months (81%) is much higher than that borrowing from family and friends over the long term (20%). This is likely linked to COVID-19 economic duress and widespread financial pressure.

The pandemic also made access to credit more difficult, as banks became more risk averse, despite a high demand for funding. Banks and other creditors required more rigorous checks and stronger guarantees and collateral requirements. Recent research indicates that WSMEs suffered to a greater extent due to poor enforcement of the land-use rights certificate, which made it harder for women entrepreneurs to validate their legal assets and provide collateral for supporting loans.

Weak access to networks and training opportunities for women entrepreneurs gave men-owned SMEs an edge in terms of dealing with the COVID-19 shock and undertaking plans and digital transformations.

---

[34]   Report on Financial Access of Women-Owned Small and Medium-Sized Enterprises In Viet Nam. ADB 2022.

Assessment of Policies, Legal and Regulatory Frameworks Supporting Women-Owned Small and Medium-Sized Enterprises

5

This chapter assesses the policy and legal framework in Viet Nam with respect to the specific barriers facing WSMEs. The analysis derives from the review of 11 policy documents and stakeholder consultations undertaken from October 2021 to January 2022.[35] Data was collected from agencies at the central level and from four provinces: Lao Cai, Northern Region; Hue City, Central Region; Lam Dong, Central Highlands; and Can Tho, Southern Region. Further details regarding government institutions involved in SME policy and implementation, and a summary of these 11 key legal and policy documents related to SMEs and WSMEs are included in Appendix 5.

Government Actions and Initiatives in Support of Women-Owned Small and Medium-Sized Enterprises

The government has been proactive in its support for SMEs, issuing and amending several major pieces of legislation since 2017. These are generally gender-neutral, with gender per se the subject of its own law.

The Law on Gender Equality (Law No. 73/2006/QH11) was the first separate legal document regulating gender equality in the Vietnamese legal system. It targets gender equality in all fields of social and family life, including politics, economy, labor, education and training, science and technology, culture, information, physical training, and sports. In 2021, a new National Gender Equality Strategy came into effect for 2021–2030. The document includes 20 targets relating to women in all aspects of socioeconomic and political life, including specific objectives for women's entrepreneurship. However, the Law on Promulgation of Legal Documents (2015) should be amended to ensure that the principle of gender equality is mainstreamed into all legal and policy documents at both national and provincial levels. Particular attention should be paid to mandating references to women in business and women-owned enterprises. The following laws should also be amended to reflect this:

---

[35] Documents reviewed: SME Law, National Gender Equality Strategy, Law on Gender Equality, Decision No. 939/QD-TTg, Law on Enterprises, Law on Investment, Resolution No. 02/NQ-CP, Resolution No. 35/NQ-CP, Resolution No. 10/NQ-TW, Resolution No. 98/NQ-CP, Resolution No. 68/NQ-CP, and several COVID-19 supporting policy documents.

- Law on Gender Equality, 2006
- Law on Organization of National Assembly, 2014
- Law on Organization of Government, 2015
- Law on Organization of Local Government, 2015

In 2017 and specific to women in business, Decision No. 939/QD-TTg (Project 939) was passed to support women's entrepreneurship during 2017–2025. It aims to raise awareness of women's enterprise development and contribute to the targets set out in the National Strategy on Gender Equality. The decision specifically referenced targets supporting 20,000 women starting a business and supporting 100,000 existing WSMEs with consulting services and enterprise training.

The government has also recently passed updated versions of business-focused legislation, such as the Law on Enterprise, the Law on Investment, and various associated resolutions (e.g., No. 02/NQ-CP, No. 35/NQ-CP, No. 10-NQ/TW, and No. 68/NQ-CP). Despite the lack of a targeted gender focus, these laws have facilitated significant gains for WSMEs (and men-owned SMEs) through simplified business regulations and mobilizing investment.

Of note is No. 04/2017/QH14 on *Support for the SME Law (SME Support Law)*. This is the most significant piece of Vietnamese legislation targeted at SMEs. It specifies measures, provisions, and responsibilities across ministries, agencies, and other government organizations. The 2017 SME Support Law is notable as the first piece of legislation to provide a clear definition of women-owned enterprises. Under Article 3, WSMEs are defined as an SME having one or more women owning at least 51% of its charter capital, and at least one woman serving as the executive director of the enterprise. This is the definition used for the analysis of GSO 2021 Economic Census data. Though the law still lacks a targeted gender focus, it has fostered significant gains for WSMEs.

On the basis of the Law on SME Support, Decree No. 80/2021/ND-CP dated 26 August 2021, the government has specified various forms of support with higher cost norms for WSMEs. These include the following:

(i)   Consulting support. WSMEs are supported for 100% of the consulting contract value but not exceeding D70 million/year per enterprise for microenterprises, reimbursement of up to 50% of the consulting contract value but not exceeding D150 million/year per enterprise for small enterprises, and reimbursement of up to 30% of the consulting contract value but not exceeding D200 million/year per enterprise for medium enterprises.

(ii)   Training support. This includes exemptions of tuition fees for employees of WSMEs who participate in training courses on start-up and business administration, and reimbursement of 100% of the costs of direct training courses for enterprises.

The MPI also issued Circular No. 06/2022/TT-BKHDT to guide the implementation of Decree No. 80/2021/ND-CP, which regulates SME-supporting agencies and organizations to prioritize funding to support WSMEs.

During 2020–2022, the government issued several business support policies to help Vietnamese enterprises overcome the difficulties that arose due to the COVID-19 pandemic (e.g., Resolution No. 42/NQ-CP, No. 84/NQ-CP, No. 68/NQ-CP/2021, No. 105/NQ-CP, and No. 11/NQ-CP/2022).[36] WSMEs benefited from such support policies to the extent that they knew about them and could access support.

During the COVID-19 period, the government implemented numerous policies to support businesses such as implementing Resolution 42/NQ-CP 2020 and offering support to those who suffered from a significant decrease in income because of the pandemic. Workers were eligible for up to D1.8 million ($77) per month and up to three months if they were forced to take unpaid leave, household businesses who earned an annual revenue of under D100 million a year ($4,260) and had to suspend business operations received D1 million ($43) per month for up to three months and employers were able to apply for an unsecured loan worth up to 50% of total region-based minimum wages of suspended employees over the suspension period up to three months at an interest rate of 0% from the Viet Nam Bank for Social Policies.[37, 38, 39]

Fiscal support for firms (estimated at around 4% of GDP in 2020) largely took the form of tax cuts and tax deferrals. In addition, a credit support package of around 4% of GDP comprising loan restructuring and interest rate reductions was also rolled out in early 2020.[40] Throughout the COVID-19 pandemic recovery, the government also implemented the National Economic Recovery Program during 2022–2023, which included additional support measures for SMEs.

It is evident that the government has taken many initiatives to support SMEs, particularly during the COVID-19 period. These initiatives are rarely, however, undertaken with a gender lens in place. The lack of a gender lens in documents is partly because of the lack of gendered data, but also because women are viewed as "addressed" through initiatives implementing the National Gender Equity Strategy. This is not a satisfactory situation. Gender is relevant and should be explicitly addressed, to some extent, in all policy documents—not just in those with gender in the title.

Applying a gender lens to all legal documents is already policy. Objective 7 (Norm 1) of the National Strategy on Gender Equality 2011–2020: *"80% by 2015 and 100% by 2020 of legal drafts will be determined as having contents related to gender equality, gender inequality or discrimination."* It is imperative that this requirement is not forgotten when drafting all new legal documents. Ideally, there would be a stage in the drafting process (at National Assembly) where alignment with the National Gender Strategy is confirmed.

---

[36]   These support policies included a reduction of payable tax (e.g., the government cut the VAT tax rate from 10% to 8%, waived the payment of 30% on corporate income tax), land rental (30% reduction on the payable amount), or loan interest (cutting the interest rate by 2% on loans with bank).

[37]   Vietanlaw. Resolution 42/NQ-CP 2020 assistance for people affected by Covid-19 pandemic.

[38]   COVID-19 Pandemic Portal of the Ministry of Health. https://covid19.gov.vn/ (in Vietnamese).

[39]   Currency unit Viet Nam Dong (D). D1 = $0.000043. Exchange rates as of May 2023.

[40]   International Monetary Fund. 2021. *Viet Nam: 2020 Article IV Consultation–Press Release; Staff Report; and Statement by the Executive Director for Vietnam.* Vol. 2021/042.

Results of Policy Implementation and Impacts on Women-Owned Small and Medium-Sized Enterprises

Central Level

As noted above, most WSMEs do not consider the legal and policy environment as discriminatory or inhibitive. This is supported by the document reviews undertaken for this report, which found no explicit gender-based discrimination in the language of legislation.

Nevertheless, findings from the WSME survey and consultations with women entrepreneurs suggest that a high proportion of WSMEs feel they are not well-supported by government policies and have not benefited from existing SME support initiatives. For example, only 48% of women owners "agreed" or "strongly agreed" that WSMEs are well-supported through national level policy (Figure 8).

This may be because businesspeople always want more support, but also the WSME survey results pointed to a lack of knowledge on existing support mechanisms available to businesses. Interviews with women business owners confirmed their limited knowledge of business support mechanisms like tax benefits, training opportunities, or preferential credit schemes. The government

Figure 8: Rates at Which Women-Owned Small and Medium-Sized Enterprises Feel Supported by National Level Government Legislation

Agree or Disagree: "WSMEs are well-supported through national government policy and programming."

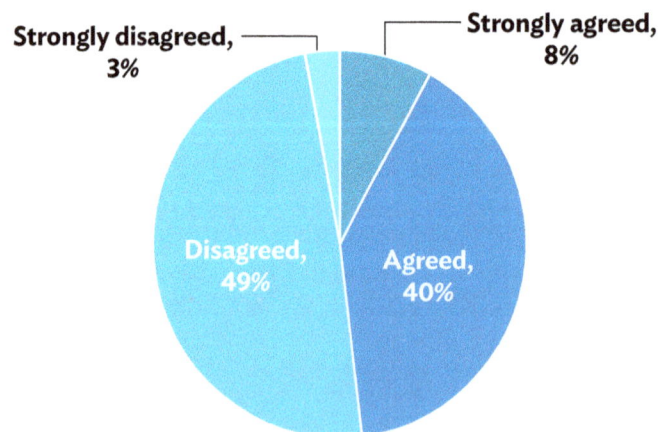

- Strongly disagreed, 3%
- Strongly agreed, 8%
- Disagreed, 49%
- Agreed, 40%

WSME = women-owned micro, small, and medium-sized enterprises.
Source: Palladium-Mekong Economics. 2022. WSME Survey (n=118).

may not be up to date in how to effectively market its own initiatives. And the government agencies at both central and provincial levels may lack of state budget to disseminate the information through social media channels such as television.

That most SME legal and policy documents do not make distinct reference to women, gender, and women-owned businesses could help explain why women do not feel well-supported by national government policy and programming. Of the 11 documents reviewed, only four specifically mention women in at least one instance (SME Support Law, 2017; National Strategy on Gender Equality 2011–2020 and the newly issued National Strategy on Gender Equality 2021–2030; Law on Gender Equality, 2006; and Decision No. 939/QD-TTg dated 30 June 2017 approving the program for supporting women in entrepreneurship during 2017–2025). In the remaining seven documents, no reference is made to "women," "WSMEs," "gender," or "female."

Most importantly, the documents reviewed align poorly with national priorities on gender equality and women's economic empowerment (WEE). For instance, several documents state that an aim of "creating favorable conditions for start-ups and innovative enterprises," but there was no link to the National Strategy for Gender Equality 2021–2030 which targets "the rate of female directors and female owners of enterprises and cooperatives will reach 27% by 2025 and 30% or higher by 2030."[41]

Article 5.5 of the Law on Investment says "the state shall treat investors equitably" but makes no specific reference to women or gender-based discrimination. A gender lens might add clarity to the definition of "equity" by adding: "the state ensures gender equity in investment activities, in access to and use of loan capital, assistance funds, land, and other resources."

Part of the challenge in integrating a gender equality perspective at all stages and levels of policy development, policymaking, and policy implementation is the insufficient scope offered by the 2015 Law on Promulgation of Legal Documents. This document states that gender equality mainstreaming is only required in policy documents directly concerning issues around gender and WEE. This is contradictory to the National Strategy on Gender Equality 2011–2020 (Objective 7, Norm 1). In addition, the Law on Gender Equality only requires gender equality mainstreaming in draft legal normative documents, and not in national or provincial policies such as socioeconomic development plans, or national and provincial target programs. This also contravenes Objective 7 (Norm 1) under the National Strategy 2011–2020.

Of those laws and policies that do address gender equality (SME Support Law, National Strategy on Gender Equality, Law on Gender Equality, and Decision No. 939/QD-TTg), inadequate attention is paid to WSMEs. For example, the Law on Gender Equality does not refer to WSMEs or women-owned household businesses nor does it specify measures to promote gender equality in relation to WSMEs or women-owned household businesses. As noted above, the 2017 SME

---

[41] https://datafiles.chinhphu.vn/cpp/files/vbpq/2021/03/28.signed.pdf (in Vietnamese).

Support Law has regulations on prioritizing support to WSMEs. The Law on Gender Equality should also include general provisions to support WSMEs.

Where women and WSME activities are highlighted, documents lack clarity on how terms are defined. For example, the Law on Gender Equality refers to prohibited acts in terms of gender-based discrimination and misogynistic business practices but offers no clear definition of what these terms mean in practice. Related to this, the associated Decree No. 125/2021/ND-CP dated 28 December 2021 specifies penalties of D3,000,000 to D5,000,000 for acts impeding or preventing men and women from setting up a business and carrying out discriminatory business activities. However, the regulations do not refer to any penalties for gender-based discrimination in terms of business support services such as access to credit, access to training services, or access to technology.

From a monitoring and evaluation perspective, few of the legal and policy documents offer associated targets or indicators that allow for impact measurement. Where indicators are specified, none mention WSMEs, making it difficult to evaluate the impact of a particular law or policy document. Useful indicators for women in business and WSME support are stipulated under the National Strategy on Gender Equality 2011–2020 (e.g., achieving by 2020, a rate of 35% of women entrepreneurs, 50% of women holding master's degrees, and women accounting for 25% of participants in government Party committees). These indicators, however, are not well linked to relevant legal documents and policies. Targets are commendable, but they should be carefully measured and reported and in all relevant legal documents. Otherwise, gender as a policy concern remains invisible.

The government is making concerted efforts to support SMEs, but there is a lack of gender focus. The country lacks a national strategic framework for women entrepreneurs and WSME development. There is also no official focal point for coordinating and promoting WSMEs at the national level.

Provincial Level

At the provincial level, sub-documents and circulars designed to implement central-level policies lack references to gender equality and WEE, and many implementing documents lack clarity or have not been drafted. In the survey of 118 provincial WSME owners, 52% reported that government SME initiatives at the local level offered support measures specifically tailored to WSMEs (Figure 9). In discussions, several WSMEs stated that while there were often positive statements of support and policy targets at the central level, not enough was being done to pass these down and act on barriers to women's entrepreneurship at the provincial level.

Many actions have been undertaken in the provinces. Since 2018, Women's Unions have allocated D194,268 million ($8.3 million) to support women establishing businesses, the Women's Entrepreneurship Day, and the National Women's Entrepreneurship Competition. At the local level, the Provincial Women's Unions have successfully mobilized inter-sector coordination from local budgets for business development.

Figure 9: Rates of Perceived Support for Women-Owned Small and Medium-Sized Enterprises at Local Government Level

Agree or Disagree: "There are local government initiatives that offer support to women-owned SMEs as distinct from men-owned SMEs."

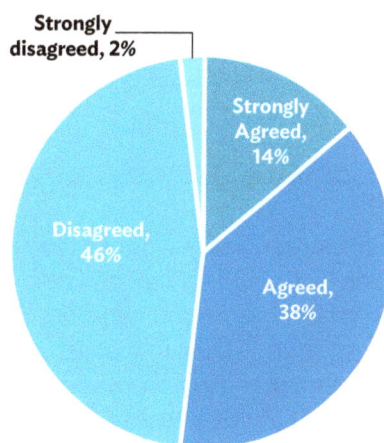

Strongly disagreed, 2%
Strongly Agreed, 14%
Disagreed, 46%
Agreed, 38%

SMEs = small and medium-sized enterprises.
Source: Palladium-Mekong Economics. 2022. WSME Survey (n=118).

Research for the White Book looked at four provinces as case studies of subnational regulations and implementation of support for WSMEs. The main takeaway is that WSME-specific funds and initiatives, and even targets, are evident in all provinces. What is lacking is a more holistic gender lens approach to drafting regulations and designing projects. Thus, outside activities specifically targeting women gender is invisible. Such activities are typically implemented by the Women's Union and other women's business associations (e.g., Viet Nam Women Entrepreneurs Council under the Viet Nam Chamber of Commerce and Industry, the Women's Association of Vietnamese Entrepreneurs, and provincial women business associations).

Lao Cai, Northern Region

In Lao Cai, the People's Committee issued Plan No. 224/KH-UBND on 11 May 2021 to implement the National Strategy on Gender Equality during 2021–2025 and up to 2030. In this plan, the province set an ambitious target for the proportion of women directors or business owners to reach at least 33% in 2025 and 35% in 2030 (currently 13%).

In addition, the Women's Union has been assigned to cooperate with the Department of Labor, Invalids and Social Affairs (DOLISA) in supporting women to create jobs and develop enterprises by providing preferential loans and communication channels for developing products and accessing new markets, particularly across the border with the People's Republic of China. The Provincial Women's Union established the Women Support Development Fund in 2013. The fund reports that it now has around 2,000 members with a total outstanding loan balance of D16 billion ($680,000).

Plan No. 224/KH-UBND also requested local agencies to implement policies to attract investment and encourage the development of industries that typically employ many women workers. The document sets out plans to improve the quality of job exchanges and labor market information, introduce and connect businesses with vocational education, and train institutions and employees on the principles of gender equality.

Thua Thien Hue, Central Region

The People's Committee in Thua Thien Hue has promulgated several plans to implement the National Strategy on Gender Equality. In the latest plan, the provincial government has set a target of at least 30% of businesses to be women-owned by 2025 (28% in 2020). In discussion with the provincial Department of Planning and Investment (DPI), the province has made good progress toward this target by promoting B2B (Business to Business) linkages through working groups, particularly in the traditional handicrafts sector where women dominate.

The province has assigned both the DPI and the DOLISA to lead on achieving targets related to gender equality, but how they will be achieved remains unclear.

The Department of Justice (DOJ) carries out regular reviews of legal and normative regulations to assess the incorporation of gender equality. However, due to their limited human resources, they can only focus on regulations specifically related to children and women. For more general business and other regulations, these reviews do not take place. There is also a lack of knowledge and technical capacity on gender issues, with only abstract guidance from the DOJ, which is difficult to use. DOJ and other officials need training in how to apply a gender lens when drafting laws and regulations.

Most programs related to gender equality in the economic sector are carried out by the Provincial Women's Union, including training programs and a credit fund for women entrepreneurs. However, their budget is limited. The Women's Union is assigned by the People's Committee to manage a credit fund of D4 billion ($170,000), which will then provide unsecured loans of around D20 million ($850) to women-owned businesses.

Lam Dong, Central Highlands

Lam Dong People's Committee issued Plan No. 2167/KH-UBND dated 12 April 2021 to implement the National Strategy on Gender Equality during 2021–2025. In this plan, the province has set a target of reaching 33% of business owners being women by 2025 (30% in 2020).

The Women's Union has implemented some activities to support gender equality, such as vocational training for women employees (25,000 women), support for preferential loan access from the Policy Bank (3,000 women), and small-scale lending schemes (2,300 women). The Provincial Women's Union also helped set up nine cooperatives and 46 cooperation groups. Lam Dong Women's Union is setting up a women entrepreneur's club.

Can Tho, Southern Region

Can Tho City issued Plan No. 103/KH-UBND dated 10 May 2021 to implement the National Strategy on Gender Equality during 2021–2030. In this plan, Can Tho City set a target of 27% of business owners being women by 2025 (26% in 2020) and 30% by 2030. To achieve this, the local government plans to set out clear steps, such as ensuring that women have full and equal access to economic resources (e.g., credit, market information, and information on laws and policies) and initiating women-targeted training in business administration and technical skills.

According to the Provincial Women's Union, however, Can Tho failed to achieve some targets under the National Strategy on Gender Equality due to difficulties associated with training women entrepreneurs and a limited budget.

In terms of business registration, the DPI claims to have simplified the process and created online registration portals to make it easier for WSMEs to register their businesses, with registration taking an average of two days to complete. The proportion of newly registered businesses online increased from 23% in 2017 to 53% in 2021. However, these are figures for combined men- and women-owned enterprises, and no gender-disaggregated data is currently available.

Impact of COVID-19 Policy Support

As the pandemic progressed, firms in Viet Nam seem to have used government support policies better, with more enterprises reporting having received some support from the government in September 2021 compared to 2020.[42]

In terms of assistance, the majority of WSMEs surveyed in Questionnaire 1.15 of the 2021 Economic Census (57%) said they had not received any COVID-19 support from the government. Many reported registering for assistance programs but not receiving any information or announcements on next steps. Figure 10 shows the ease of access for those WSMEs who did benefit from eight different types of assistance. Strict eligibility requirements also appear to have been a barrier with newly established businesses not permitted to apply for support. Those that did receive government assistance reported temporary tax relief, wage allowances for employees, and rent support for business premises. However, many WSMEs interviewed for this report said there was a lack of supporting information and complex administrative procedures to complete before assistance was granted.

---

[42]   World Bank. 2022. *No Time to Waste: The Challenges and Opportunities of Cleaner Trade for Viet Nam*. Taking Stock © World Bank, Ha Noi. https://openknowledge.worldbank.org/entities/publication/b65ddccc-a294-5838-9f36-841fdc849371 License: CC BY 3.0 IGO."

Figure 10: Women-Owned Businesses Evaluation on Ease of Access to Support Policies, 2020
(%)

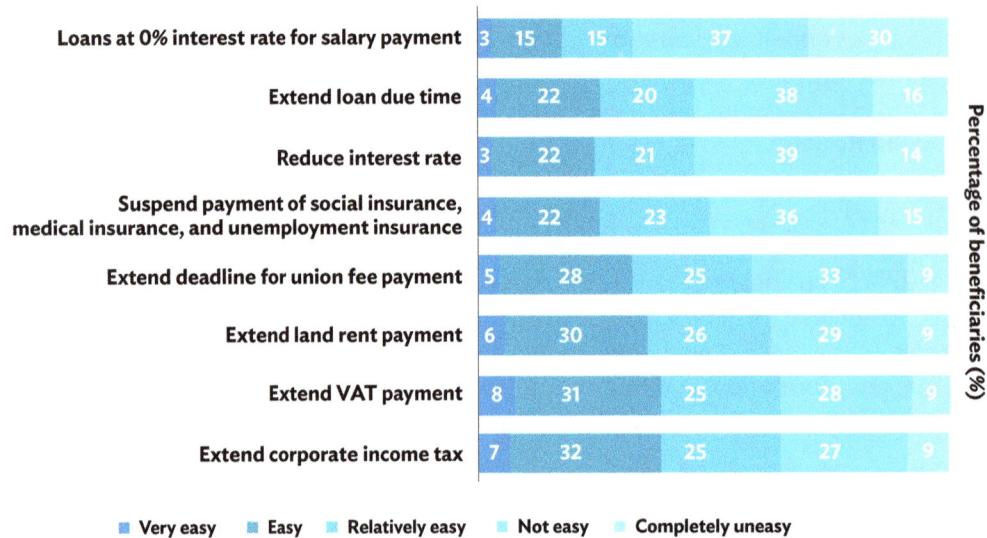

Policy	Very easy	Easy	Relatively easy	Not easy	Completely uneasy
Loans at 0% interest rate for salary payment	3	15	15	37	30
Extend loan due time	4	22	20	38	16
Reduce interest rate	3	22	21	39	14
Suspend payment of social insurance, medical insurance, and unemployment insurance	4	22	23	36	15
Extend deadline for union fee payment	5	28	25	33	9
Extend land rent payment	6	30	26	29	9
Extend VAT payment	8	31	25	28	9
Extend corporate income tax	7	32	25	27	9

Percentage of beneficiaries (%)

■ Very easy ■ Easy ■ Relatively easy ■ Not easy ■ Completely uneasy

VAT = value-added tax.

Source: VCCI–USAID. 2021. PCI Survey.

Of those who received government support, 13% were businesses having fewer than 10 employees and 37% were SMEs.[43]

Women-owned businesses had positive perceptions and agreed more with response activities of local governments compared to men-owned businesses. Regarding access to government support policies, the easiest to access was deferral of corporate income tax and value-added tax (VAT) payments. The most difficult to access was borrowing at 0% for paying workers. Finally, women entrepreneurs are less optimistic about business for the next two years. Only 22% predict their businesses will increase and 9% predict it will "definitely" increase. At the same time, 25% of men-owned businesses predict there is a possible positive increase in business and 10% predict a definite increase.

Box 2 details the initiatives taken to mitigate COVID-19 impacts across the four provinces. In Lao Cai, WSMEs reported a government support program that helped businesses with marketing challenges during the pandemic. Women were encouraged to develop websites and promote their products on e-commerce sites and television. Moreover, subsidies were provided for postage and packaging costs to support businesses with online transactions. This is an example of effective COVID-19 policy support that helped WSMEs to adapt during the pandemic, simultaneously addressing one of the main functional barriers to their business growth: access to technology.

Overall, COVID-19 exacerbated gender barriers, forcing WSMEs to shut down to a greater extent than men-owned businesses. The reduced ability to adapt their businesses through technology and increased household burdens due to the

---

[43]   NEU–JICA. 2020.

Box 2: Provincial Government's COVID-19 Support to Women-Owned Small and Medium-Sized Enterprises

Provincial government agencies implemented several specific plans to help ease the negative effects of the COVID-19 pandemic.

Lao Cai Province

The government of Lao Cai Province issued Plan 303/KH-UBND dated 16 July 2021. This plan is the basis for implementing central government Resolution 68/NQ-CP on support to employees and employers facing difficulties due to COVID-19. Local agencies such as the Department of Tax and the Department of Labor, Invalids and Social Affairs (DOLISA) actively disclosed business support information about policies to enterprises through direct telephone calls or via web portals. These policies included tax breaks and preferential short-term business loans. Business adaptation training was also made available to support enterprises with online marketing and e-commerce.

Results updated to December 2021 show that 1,359 enterprises received social insurance-based tax relief, amounting to a cumulative business saving of D8.9 billion ($380,000) across the province, and 11 enterprises received preferential short-term business loans to cover immediate business expenses and staff salaries. These loans totaled D238 million ($10,000) across the province. Business support data disaggregated by gender is not available.

Thua Thien Hue Province

On 14 July 2020, the People's Committee of Thua Thien Hue issued Plan No.166/KH-UBND to implement Resolution 84/NQ-CP on tasks and solutions to overcome difficulties in business operations due to COVID-19. Information about business support policies and their status of implementation were posted on the DOLISA website. These figures show that as of December 2021, there were 184 businesses receiving social insurance breaks with a cumulative business saving of D552 million ($23,000) and 154 enterprises receiving COVID-19 business loans for a total value of D1 billion ($42,600). While gender-disaggregated data is again unavailable, unlike other provinces, the Women's Union actively supervised the implementation of these support policies.

Lam Dong Province

In Lam Dong, the People's Committee issued Plan No.4848/KH-UBND on 14 July 2021 to implement Resolution 68/NQ-CP on support to employees and employers facing difficulties due to COVID-19. The plan assigned specific tasks to local agencies for implementing support policies to employers and employees. However, no update on the results of these proposed support policies could be found. Very few WSMEs consulted in Lam Dong were aware of COVID-19 business support policies and none reported receiving any support.

Can Tho City

Can Tho City did not have specific guidance or a plan for implementing Resolution 68/ND-CP on COVID-19 support. However, according to a report from DOLISA, Can Tho City gave COVID-19 loan support to 3,678 employers totaling D418 billion ($17.8 million)[a] by December 2021. This support accounted for nearly 80% of the approved budget for COVID-19 business assistance in the province. Business support data disaggregated by gender is not available.

In discussions with WSMEs, respondents said tax relief support was available in principle but felt this was not properly disclosed by provincial tax authorities and few businesses benefited.

---

[a] Viet Nam Dong (D). D1 = $0.000043. Exchange rates correct as of May 2023.

Source: Consultations with the provincial government agencies in Lao Cai, Thua Thien Hue, Lam Dong, and Can Tho from late 2021 to early 2022.

closure of schools and childcare facilities are just two examples of how WSMEs were more affected by and continue to be affected by the pandemic and its continuing outcomes. Added to this was inaccessible information on available government support initiatives. COVID-19 support was disjointed with programs available in some places and not others, available to some businesses but not all. Many WSMEs who may have been eligible for assistance did not apply due to lack of information and awareness.

6 International Experience, Best Practice

Compared to many countries, including others in Southeast Asia, Viet Nam performs relatively well on measures of gender equality and women's economic empowerment (WEE). Vietnamese women have high labor force participation rates, are equal to men in the eyes of the law and women-owned businesses exhibit broadly similar characteristics to men-owned businesses in terms of size, revenue, and profits. Nevertheless, WSMEs are still faced with significant and deep-rooted barriers to their growth and development. With approximately only one-fifth of all businesses owned by women, Viet Nam is still far from gender parity. There are many examples of successful and innovative policy initiatives to promote women's entrepreneurship and support WSMEs. In general, policy support works best when it is contextualized and adopts a multi-stakeholder approach, engaging not just women as an isolated group, but also men, government institutions, and all realms of political and socioeconomic life.

This chapter surveys policy initiatives in other countries to see how they address the challenges of women doing business, with a view to identifying some that are relevant to Viet Nam.

Access to Credit

There are a number of well-tested policy measures to facilitate better access to finance for WSMEs, typically involving earmarking funds to be distributed specifically to women entrepreneurs through loans or grants and better engaging sources of private sector finance. Innovative mechanisms for distributing such funds through microfinance schemes and fintech platforms have been successful in simplifying procedures and increasing the amount of finance available to WSMEs.

Knowing your market and your customer is critical for financial institutions to improve WSMEs' access to finance. Specifically, making WSMEs a distinct group rather than an extension of existing retail or commercial businesses and segmenting WSMEs into different subgroups to offer them a set of holistic products. These measures would include core professional products and a link to personal products making WSMEs a separate group and ensuring that credit processes, underwriting standards, and delivery models can be differentiated for WSMEs. Such a "distinct group" approach, however, requires gender-disaggregated data across many measures.

Examples from Within the Association of Southeast Asian Nations

Since 2010, Malaysia has made significant progress toward collecting gender-disaggregated financial data. Financial service providers are required to collect and report gender-disaggregated data on credit and deposit facilities. The data collected involves both supply- and demand-side data and includes metrics such as the number of women borrowers, the number of women depositors, and the number of women-owned loan accounts at commercial banks. This data is then submitted to Bank Negara Malaysia (Malaysia's central bank) where it is then cross-referenced against the national ID system to disaggregate various indicators by gender. Demand-side data is also collected to complement supply-side data. Every three years, Bank Negara Malaysia conducts a general demand-side financial inclusion survey to identify respondents' gender.[44] Such gender-disaggregated data allows for the accommodation of well-informed policy development and implementation. The use of technology can help facilitate the movement toward gender-disaggregated financial data. For example, GFI Fintech Sdn Bhd (data technology company that specializes in profiling technology for the finance industry) employs an innovative credit risk assessment system known as GFI. This system uses psychographic variables to gauge an individual's creditworthiness. By harnessing the power of machine learning, artificial intelligence, behavioral science, and psychometrics, GFI accurately predicts the likelihood of a person defaulting on their financing obligations. Women account for 60% of GFI's staff and 40% of GFI test-takers. GFI aims to help all women, including entrepreneurs, business owners, employed women, and women at home.[45]

SME Bank, a state-owned commercial bank licensed in 2020, administers the Cambodia Women Entrepreneurs Scheme, a COVID-19 recovery initiative that provides loans at favorable rates to support women-owned SMEs. Eligible businesses can borrow at an interest rate of 6.5% per annum, which is lower than the prevailing market rates, and benefit from deferred payment and extended repayment terms (footnote 45).

Another instance from the region is the Banque Franco-Lao of the Lao People's Democratic Republic, which was established in 2008 as a joint venture between BRED Banque Populaire, a French bank, and BCEL- Banque Pour Le Commerce Exterieur Lao Public, a leading Lao bank. In 2015, the bank launched a financing facility for small and medium enterprises (SMEs) with 50% risk taken on by the bank. In 2016, the bank introduced the Women's Market Program, with the objective of expanding finance access for women entrepreneurs by providing a combination of financial and nonfinancial services. Through this program, the bank has been able to reduce collateral requirements for women-owned businesses and offer collateral-free loans to eligible women entrepreneurs on a case-by-case basis (footnote 45).

---

[44]   UN Secretary-General's Special Advocate for Inclusive Finance for Development. *Collecting and Using Gender-Disaggregated Data for Financial Policymaking*.

[45]   Diana Bialus, Le Thanh Tam, Nguyen Thi Thu Hien, and Chu Hong Minh. 2022. Financial Access of Women-Owned Small and Medium-Sized Enterprises in Viet Nam. *ADB Southeast Asia Working Paper Series No. 22.* Manila: ADB.

A fourth example is the Inclusive Lending for Aspiring Women Program, introduced by the Development Bank of the Philippines in 2015. This business loan program aims to assist women entrepreneurs to scale up their businesses. It enables businesses led by women and with women ownership to qualify for simplified lending procedures and requirements. The program includes a flexible collateral policy allowing for alternative forms of collateral and customized repayment schedules tailored to the specific needs of the borrowers.

Examples from Outside the Association of Southeast Asian Nations

Box 3 shows how gender-disaggregated data collection was integrated into the Spanish Gender Law. This policy allows banks and financial institutions to collect and analyze gender data to prove to their boards that investing in the women's market is good for business and why they should continue to support investment in this segment. In addition, the provision of products customized to cater to the unique needs of WSMEs has been enhanced by using this disaggregated data.

Box 3: Gender-Disaggregated Data Collection. A Good Practice Example from Spain and the United Kingdom

Under Spanish legislation, the Gender Equality Law (Article 20) states that public authorities must systematically include variables for gender in their statistics, surveys, and data. The law is implemented alongside a National Statistical Plan that was drafted with input from a gender impact assessment that is updated and re-drafted every four years. These statistics feed into the database "Mujeres en Cifras" (Women in Figures) managed by the specially assigned Institute of Women for Equal Opportunities (IWEO), under the Ministry of Health, Social Services and Equality. Mujeres en Cifras contains more than 300 indicators, showing the situation of women in different sectors, including firm ownership, size, revenue, and equity. Furthermore, IWEO collaborates closely with the National Institute of Statistics to jointly publish the annual report, "Mujeres y Hombres en España" (Women and Men in Spain). This provides up-to-date information and statistics about men and women in the main social and economic areas. Finally, the institute promotes and participates in the design of public policies aimed at improving the employability and permanence in employment of women and their professional promotion to positions of responsibility and management.

Launched in 2019, the Investing in Women Code by the British Business Bank and funded by the Government of the United Kingdom is a pledge to boost the progress of women in entrepreneurship by enhancing their access to financial resources, tools, and services. The signatories' commitments include nominating a member of the senior leadership team responsible for supporting equality and adopting internal practices to improve women entrepreneurs' access to finance needed to start and grow successful businesses. One of the main strategies is to enhance the transparency of financial institutions regarding their support for women entrepreneurs. Signatories are required to provide data to the Department for Business and Trade nominated industry body to be published annually on an aggregated and anonymized basis. As part of this effort, the code mandates the collection of data on financing activities for women entrepreneurs by financial services firms, to be reported annually by the Treasury.[a]

[a] British Business Bank. Advancing female entrepreneurship; United Kingdom Business Angels Association. Investing in Women Code; The Indonesian Conditional Cash Transfer Program.

Source: OECD. OECD Toolkit for Mainstreaming and Implementing Gender Equality. British Business Bank. Advancing female entrepreneurship; United Kingdom Business Angels Association.

Assistance to Establish and Transform Household Businesses to Formal Enterprises

Transforming household businesses to formal enterprises involves a transaction cost, as well as higher corporate income tax rates, increased accounting and financial compliance, the need for labor contracts, and more frequent inspections. The associated financial burden means that household businesses are generally reluctant to take the step of transforming into a more formal enterprise. As such, government policies that reduce this source of friction become necessary to make the decision more favorable for WSMEs.

Examples from Within the Association of Southeast Asian Nations

The MyCOID System (Malaysia's Corporate Identity Number) in Malaysia is an online company registration and incorporation service launched by the Companies Commission of Malaysia in 2016. The system uses a single identification number as a reference for all registrations and transactions with government agencies, eliminating the need for multiple serial numbers for public dealings and internal references. The MyCOID System has streamlined the process of company incorporation, making it easy, efficient, and "hassle-free." The benefits of this system are numerous, including facilitating the business community, promoting interagency collaboration, and enhancing the overall efficiency of public transactions with relevant government agencies.[46]

Singapore has also established a similar system called the BizFile System, developed by the Accounting and Corporate Regulatory Authority (ACRA) in 2004. BizFile is a secure and cost-effective online platform that serves as a comprehensive directory for all business transactions in the country. It offers a range of services, including choosing a company name, registration, updating company information, annual filing, purchasing a Special Unique Entity Number, and renewing or closing a business. These services previously required a lengthy and cumbersome process, but with BizFile, business owners can complete them conveniently from their homes or offices. Since its launch, the ACRA BizFile System has been a tremendous success, processing over one million transactions annually.[47]

Viet Nam already has a network of one-stop-shops, but these can be leveraged to do more than help complete registrations. An optional "assistance menu" could be offered, such as help drafting a business plan, preparing bank loan applications, or learning how to do e-marketing. In this way, those setting up a business can be targeted for more effective capacity building.

---

[46]   MyCOID SSM System – Online Company Incorporation.
[47]   Understanding ACRA BizFile System?

Examples from Outside the Association of Southeast Asian Nations

The one-stop-shop solutions developed by both Croatia and Catalonia were notably successful. These shops allowed WSMEs to access crucial information, create networks and market links, and participate in training, advice, and mentorship programs, all under one website.

Before the digital Catalonian One-Stop-Shop was launched in 2014, entrepreneurs had to go through three levels of administration to start a business. The one-stop-shop streamlined the processes by working with relevant administrations and business organizations. The website features a "guide procedures search" tool that provides information about procedures for any activity, free of cost. At the end of 2017, 76% of administrative procedures were processed digitally, compared to 37% in 2014. In 2018, 916 Catalonian city councils were fully integrated into the one-stop-shop.[48]

Similarly, in Croatia, as part of a broader project called e-Croatia, which aimed to modernize public services, Croatia created HITRO.hr, a digital one-stop-shop service. Unnecessary procedures and permits were reviewed and cut to simplify the business registration process. In Croatia, an entrepreneur needed to plan on 40 days to start a firm. The new service has reduced this to three to five days. HITRO.hr received the Good Practice Label award at the 2009 European e-Government Awards.[49]

Develop Entrepreneurship Skills through Training Courses and Mentoring

Mentoring relationships between experienced and novice entrepreneurs can also have valuable benefits for new and potential entrepreneurs. These relationships can increase awareness of entrepreneurship, help develop entrepreneurial attitudes, and provide support and encouragement during business creation and development. The key to a successful mentoring relationship is the quality of the match between the novice entrepreneur (i.e., mentee) and the experienced entrepreneur (i.e., mentor).

Examples from Within the Association of Southeast Asian Nations

In the Asia and Pacific region, through the Asia-Pacific Micro, Small, and Medium Enterprise Trade Coalition, the Asian Trade Centre Foundation partnered with the UPS (United Parcel Service) Foundation to create the Asia Women Exporters' Mentorship Program which provided WSMEs in the Philippines and wider Asia and Pacific region with technical knowledge, digital entrepreneurial skills, and expert guidance to support their business growth, enhance export competitiveness, and broaden their participation in cross-border trade.[50]

---

[48]   Gencat https://www.interregeurope.eu/find-policy-solutions/stories/the-one-stop-shop-as-a-driving-force-to-sme-smart-regulation.

[49]   https://joinup.ec.europa.eu/collection/egovernment/document/hitrohr-croatian-one-stop-shop-hitrohr.

[50]   https://about.ups.com/us/en/newsroom/press-releases/diversity-equity-inclusion/ups-programme-to-empower-women-entrepreneurs-in-asia-enhance-business-export-capabilities-ph.html.

Examples from Outside the Association of Southeast Asian Nations

Evidence suggests that entrepreneurship training has a positive impact on participants in terms of the likelihood of starting up a business (see Boxes 6 and 7). For example, evidence from the United Kingdom confirms that women and men who receive entrepreneurship training through a government program are 4% more likely to start a business than those who do not participate in training. Such training and mentorships schemes are also important in fostering strong business networks and B2B (Business to Business) connections.

Assistance in Technology Acquisition and Technology Development

Digital platforms offer a chance to close entrenched gaps in access to jobs, assets, and markets. The IFC-led Digital2Equal initiative brought together leading technology companies operating in the online marketplace and helped expand opportunities for women entrepreneurs. The objective was to provide women with the necessary technological skills to participate in the platform economy.

Examples from Within the Association of Southeast Asian Nations

There are a variety of platforms, each with a different purpose, whether that be e-commerce, ridesharing, financial services, data collection, or employment. Digital2Equal targets these online platforms and helps them become more gender aware. The Southeast Asia-based marketplace platform Lazada, for instance, launched the "Mompreneur" program to offer financial and nonfinancial support to help mothers start and grow their businesses online. Following a successful pilot in the Philippines, Lazada intends to scale out the Mompreneur program to other parts of Southeast Asia.[51]

Examples from Outside the Association of Southeast Asian Nations

Esty, a global e-commerce platform company, supports women-owned businesses in starting up e-commerce sales and growth through online resources, which include an e-commerce sellers' handbook that has regulatory information about e-commerce transactions, training videos, and webinars. The platform company also offers online chat forums that are available 24 hours, seven days a week for Etsy entrepreneurs on various topics such as sales, copyright protection, and product development.[52] A similar policy intervention which mandates online platforms to be more conscious of WSMEs and how they leverage and extend their own capacities may be relevant to Viet Nam.

---

[51] Lazada empowers mothers by supporting "Mompreneurs."
[52] APEC and USAID Women-Owned Businesses in Cross-Border E-Commerce—A Diagnostic Toolkit.

Access to Information, Capacities, and Confidence

Public policy can help women overcome skill barriers through entrepreneurship training, coaching, and mentoring. There is a growing trend for policymakers to focus such programs on developing skills that would support business growth. These programs typically aim to increase know-how about starting and operating a business, as well as providing formal and informal networking opportunities.

Examples from Within the Association of Southeast Asian Nations

Maxis, a communications company in Malaysia, launched the eKelas Usahawan program to help women entrepreneurs in rural areas establish a stronger digital footprint and expand their businesses. The program provides training modules on various aspects of digital marketing, such as digital photography, advertising, social media marketing, and digital payments. Since its launch in 2021, eKelas Usahawan trained over 1,000 entrepreneurs and helped them enhance their digital presence.[53]

Social attitudes and cultural views still tend to exert a negative influence on women's self-confidence and their desire to start a business. The goal of policy and communication campaigns should be to raise awareness about the potential of entrepreneurship and to increase women's motivation for business creation and development.

The WeEmpowerAsia program by UN Women is supporting this effort by providing the WeRise toolkit and training to support women entrepreneurs in Indonesia and Thailand. The program helps women overcome gender-based obstacles, assess their financial requirements, secure funding, enhance assertiveness, and empower other women to succeed.[54]

Examples from Outside the Association of Southeast Asian Nations

Role models play a crucial role in developing entrepreneurial spirit and have demonstrated an ability to impact an individual's entrepreneurial propensity, including through positive representations and stories in the media, direct interactions, and learning material and case studies used in entrepreneurship education and training programs.[55] This could also include positive role models for men, promoting positive masculinity. For example, men who are supportive of their wives in business, who see the benefits of it at the household level, and in their children.

---

53   Maxis' eKelas Usahawan continues to attract entrepreneurs in developing stronger digital skills and presence.
54   UN Women. "WeRise" together with Indonesia's female entrepreneurs.
55   Source: We-Fi. 2021. 2021 Annual Report.

There are several examples of successful ambassador programs, particularly in the European Union (Box 5). These initiatives emphasize the need to ensure only a low level of commitment is required to incentivize women entrepreneurs to become ambassadors. It is also important for any such program to be diverse and relatable, promoting women entrepreneurs from different backgrounds.

In Viet Nam, the Women's Union undertakes similar confidence, awareness-raising, and networking initiatives for women doing business. These can be expanded and made more effective by adapting what has worked in other countries.

Preferential Tax and Regulatory Regimes

There are a numerous SME regulations that specifically target women that can be drawn upon as a source of inspiration for policies in Viet Nam.

Maternity, paternity, and parental leave systems are important tools for supporting women's participation in the labor market, including self-employment. However, the crucial issue almost always neglected in these policies is their application for women-owned and women-led businesses. For instance, who leads or at least manages business operations during maternity leave?

Examples from Within the Association of Southeast Asian Nations

While there have been implementation challenges due to different interpretations of the intended scope of the directive across member states, this is the first time a maternity allowance has been granted to self-employed workers at the European Union level. The provision of childcare (e.g., daycare sites), and tax exemptions and allowances for parents to pay for childcare also encourage women's participation in the labor market (Box 4). An example from within the region is the Program Keluarga Harapan (PKH), a childcare subsidy program launched by the Government of Indonesia in 2007. This program provides a monthly cash transfer to low-income families, including those with women entrepreneurs, to help them cover the costs of childcare.[56] However, few of these measures are aimed at women entrepreneurs directly. Examples of measures that governments could take in this area to support entrepreneurs directly are the inclusion of childcare in business start-up training or other support programs.

---

[56]   The Indonesian Conditional Cash Transfer Program.

**Box 4: Improving Women's Labor Force Participation
through Childcare Provisions**

OneSky is an organization that partners with communities in Viet Nam to provide high-quality care and early childhood education training to caregivers. The organization was founded in the People's Republic of China (PRC) in 1998 with the aim of bringing responsive care to infants living in child welfare institutions. Their team of early childhood development experts trained caregivers to ensure that the youngest and most vulnerable children received the best possible start in life. In 2011, the Government of the PRC invited OneSky to train every child welfare worker in the country, and the program has since reached over 200,000 children across 31 provinces.

OneSky's success in the PRC led to the expansion of the program across Asia, including in Viet Nam. In Viet Nam, OneSky focuses on providing support to marginalized young children whose parents work in the country's industrial zones. Through their Childcare Provider Training program, OneSky partners with national and provincial governments to train independent childcare providers working in these zones. These women have traditionally received limited recognition, resources, and training, but through OneSky's program, they become empowered as skilled professionals and are able to provide high-quality care to young Vietnamese children.

A 2020 study found that OneSky's program has improved the quality of childcare and early childhood development outcomes in Viet Nam. As a result, the Viet Nam Ministry of Education and Training has invited OneSky to scale the program nationally, and the organization is now working to build government capacity to implement their training program to reach all Vietnamese children with access to quality home-based childcare. Overall, OneSky's approach in Viet Nam is centered around empowering caregivers and improving the quality of care for young children living on the margins, ensuring that they are safe, nourished, and stimulated in childcare settings.

Source: OneSky's program providing Childcare Provisions in Viet Nam (https://onesky.org/what-we-do-2/in-vietnam/).

Examples from Outside the Association of Southeast Asian Nations

One of the rare exceptions to the problem of an absentee entrepreneur can be seen in Austria, where the Betriebshilfe (Business Continuation Aid) was introduced as a means of providing a qualified replacement if the entrepreneur is "temporarily unavailable," including due to an accident or maternity leave. Similar measures are also available in Belgium (i.e., the Flying Entrepreneurs scheme) and Spain (i.e., the "interim contract"). To address this challenge, the European Union issued a Directive in 2010 (Directive 2010/41/EU) that seeks to improve the protection of self-employed women workers and assisting spouses or life partners of self-employed workers, including during maternity.

Access to Markets

Examples from Within the Association of Southeast Asian Nations

While no member countries of the Association of Southeast Asian Nations (ASEAN) have passed laws specifically supporting Gender-Responsive Procurement, some governments have implemented preferential treatment clauses that could be applied to WSMEs as an initial means of access to more gender-responsive procurement legislation. Preferential treatment in public procurement involves setting specific rules that allow specific criteria to be used for a particular target group. For example, the Philippines has adjusted for price differences by providing targeted groups with the opportunity to be awarded a contract even if their proposed offer is more expensive than other bids.[57]

In Indonesia, the government has established regulations to incentivize and support SMEs. One notable provision requires that 40% of government procurement of goods and services must come from cooperatives or SMEs. The government also provides structured down payments to SMEs and cooperatives according to contract value: 100% for contracts less than Rp50 million ($3,400), 50% for contracts worth Rp50 million to Rp200 million ($3,400 to $13,600), and 30% for contracts worth Rp200 million to Rp2.5 billion ($13,600 to $170,000).[58] While the regulation does not directly target women-owned businesses, it could be adapted to support WSMEs (footnote 63).

Examples from Outside the Association of Southeast Asian Nations

In Senegal, regulations were drafted and adopted to integrate a gender dimension into the public procurement process, and civil servants were trained on integrating the gender dimension into public procurement. These actions catalyzed WSME access to the universe of government contracts and built the capacity of WSMEs to handle these kinds of contracts.

This was a meaningful intervention, as the government is often the largest purchaser of products and services in many countries. Public procurement comprises over 30% in developing countries, of which women-led enterprises supply approximately 1%.[59] Government officials are often not aware of the capabilities of women bidders and the obstacles they face.

---

[57]   ADB and UN Women. 2022. *Gender Responsive Procurement in Asia and the Pacific*. Manila.
[58]   Currency unit Indonesian Rupiah (Rp). Rp1 = $0.0067.
[59]   International Trade Center. 2014. Empowering Women through Public Procurement. Geneva.

Box 5: One-Stop-Shop Services for Women-Owned Small and Medium-Sized Enterprises. A Good Practice Example from the European Union

The WeGATE website is a one-stop-shop for women entrepreneurs that has three main functions. First, it acts as an information hub for women entrepreneurs who are looking to start or are already operating a business. For example, women entrepreneurs can find information on business creation, finance and funding, policy and legal information, legislation and taxation, business development, regional markets, innovative research, good practice examples, case studies, and profiles of successful role models. Second, the website provides information and links to where women can access local entrepreneurship training programs, networks, and advice and mentoring programs. Third, the website acts as an online platform for networking for users who register, connecting aspiring and successful women entrepreneurs and other support providers. The website was launched in 2016 with content available in English, German, and French and navigation available in all official languages of the European Union. The online portal has so far registered 268 users (public profiles) across a range of sectors and countries.

This portal offers easy to access support. The key to its long-term success will be the active engagement of users (women entrepreneurs and support providers) and continuously updating information and links to national and regional programs and networks. For more information, see: https://wegate.eu/.

Source: WEGATE, European Union.

Box 6: Women's Entrepreneurship Ambassador Program. A Good Practice Example from Sweden

In 2008, the Government of Sweden launched their Women's Entrepreneurship Ambassadors program, intending to (i) increase the visibility of women entrepreneurship, (ii) inspire women entrepreneurship through personal stories and role models, (iii) make it easier for women to identify with entrepreneurial role models, (iv) encourage more women to view entrepreneurship as a potential career, and (v) help women address their entrepreneurial challenges by sharing their experiences. Organizers select a program ambassador to represent each Swedish region with a particular emphasis placed on creating a diverse group of ambassadors in terms of ethnicity, age, industry, company size, and geographic region. Ambassadors undertake activities to promote women's entrepreneurship such as speaking in schools, developing networks for women in business, and running coaching and advice sessions for potential women entrepreneurs. The Ambassador Program has helped to facilitate women's entrepreneurship in Sweden, involving approximately 2,000 women entrepreneurs and reaching 170,000 women.

Source: OECD. The Better Entrepreneurship Policy Tool.

Box 7: Women-Focused Business Skills Training. A Good Practice Example from France

As part of the Women's Entrepreneurship Plan launched in 2013, the Government of France offered a scheme with three main pillars of support: (i) improving information dissemination to women entrepreneurs on available public support, (ii) providing individual support to entrepreneurs (e.g., mentoring, networking), and (iii) improving access to finance for women entrepreneurs.

The first pillar aims to improve communication about entrepreneurship by strengthening the education system, supporting promotional events such as the Entrepreneurship Awareness Week, and the launch of a new website, which provides information and links to available support programs (e.g., training, mentoring). The second pillar boosts individual support for women entrepreneurs with the creation of 14 regional support networks that provide mentoring to women entrepreneurs. The third pillar aims at increasing access to finance and includes meetings and networking events for entrepreneurs, which are regularly arranged with banks and financial networks. The government also helps women entrepreneurs receive loans through loan guarantees and set the ceiling at €45,000 in 2015.

Some of these networks offer general support, while others offer tailored support for specific groups such as innovative women entrepreneurs or older women entrepreneurs. One of the main objectives of these networks is to strengthen support for women entrepreneurs in rural areas.

In its first year, the initiative mobilized a network of 130 women entrepreneurs and reached 2,600 young women who were interested in becoming entrepreneurs. Within two years, there had been 600 promotional events and 3,095 newly created jobs.

The key to the success of this initiative is its integrated approach that covers pre-start-up, start-up, and business development activities. Thus, the three pillars reinforce each other because people can move through the different stages of support as their business project develops.

Source: OECD. The Better Entrepreneurship Policy Tool.

Assistance for Innovation and Access to Business Premises and Production Space

Government incubators are one way to provide innovation support alongside functional business premises to WSMEs. Incubators demonstrably improve business and digital skills, while supporting business growth potential as they connect firms to an extended network of other firms and investors, allowing WSMEs to circumvent existing barriers.

Examples from Within the Association of Southeast Asian Nations

An example is Simona Ventures, an Indonesian-based platform that supports women entrepreneurs. Their mission is to provide women founders with end-to-end support to build their business, enabling them to compete in the male-dominated start-up community. This support comes in the form of networking and education so companies that are being founded or led by women can secure funding.[60]

---

[60]   Mulia, K. 2019. Indonesia-Based Simona Ventures and Digitaraya Team Up to Support Women-Led Startups. *KrAsia*. 29 March; Simona Ventures.

Examples from Outside ASEAN

In Pakistan, Women Entrepreneurs Finance Initiative (We-Fi) supported a World Bank investment readiness training program that trained and equipped incubators to develop products, services, and approaches tailored to WSMEs. This provided a safe business premise, where women entrepreneurs were given the necessary space to raise seed funding, while providing the requisite training facilities to guide women entrepreneurs on processes to better innovate. The project was replicated in Iraq and Jordan in 2022 and was instrumental in creating an inclusive entrepreneurial ecosystem for women entrepreneurs in the region. In addition to its other efforts, We-Fi has provided support to the Women's Finance Exchange (WFX), an initiative by ADB that seeks to enhance financial inclusion for women in the region. The WFX accomplishes this by promoting innovation in financial solutions, such as organizing hackathons and using sandbox technology to assist financial institutions and their women borrowers.[61]

Assistance to Small and Medium-Sized Enterprises Participating in Value Chains and Business Clusters

Public policy initiatives typically bring entrepreneurs and business service professionals together by linking those with a common background. Shared characteristics can quickly build bonds and trust. These networks are also important sites of knowledge dissemination, allowing entrepreneurs to share information about business support opportunities and funding.

Isolating women from mainstream business service providers and other stakeholders from other communities can occur as a result of separate networks for women entrepreneurs and women-targeted dissemination activities. It is important to build bridges with people and support providers outside the network. A common approach in the examples below is to create networks around other policy interventions such as training or other business development services. There are plenty of examples of such schemes from across the world which Viet Nam could use as a template for success.

Examples from Within the Association of Southeast Asian Nations

Established in 2014, the ASEAN Women Entrepreneurs' Network (AWEN) serves as a platform for women entrepreneurs to exchange knowledge, experiences, and best practices. AWEN fosters a network among women's organizations in the private sector, as well as women's ministries and agencies. Members benefit from training, mentoring, and networking opportunities. In February 2022, AWEN collaborated with the International Labour Organization (ILO) to organize a virtual regional networking event for women entrepreneurs operating small businesses in

---

[61]   ADB. Women's Finance Exchange.

the ASEAN region. The event brought together women entrepreneurs to create new business connections and to provide motivation and inspiration for staying resilient during and after the COVID-19 crisis.[62]

Examples from Outside the Association of Southeast Asian Nations

An international example is the Club of United Businesses (CUB), an Australian leadership community and networking service that runs tailored social experiences, roundtables, and education events aimed at women within the business community.

---

[62]   ILO. Women entrepreneurs connect across ASEAN.

7   Conclusions and Recommendations

This White Book has explored the question of why women own and manage only 20% of Vietnamese SMEs and only 11% of large enterprises. Women own 1-in-5 SMEs, and those they do own are on average smaller than men-owned SMEs. The White Book research has found that a large part of the explanation for this imbalanced ownership is that informal biases and prejudices (of both men and women) reinforce societal norms that women should not be business leaders. In other words, women doing business in Viet Nam do face particular and exceptional barriers compared to men, even though those barriers are typically not codified in law.

This White Book does not recommend price-distorting subsidization of WSMEs. That includes low-interest loan schemes, lower taxes, lower land rent, or subsidized production spaces only for WSMEs. The Law on Gender Equality, for example, makes general reference to WSMEs in equally accessing information, capital, markets, and labor sources, although few specific regulations are in place, and they have complicated instructions and procedures making them difficult to implement. The recommendations in this White Book do, however, support a level business playing field for men and women that is equal in terms of tax obligations, loan terms, and interest rates. The recommendations are aimed at encouraging women to be ambitious and acquire the knowledge and capacities needed to access opportunities equally.

In the future, ministries, localities, and associations should continue to promote the implementation of support policies for WSMEs as stipulated in Decree No. 80/2021/ND-CP and prioritize allocating resources to support WSMEs as per Circular No. 06/2022/TT-BKHDT of the Ministry of Planning and Investment (MPI). In the long term, the government could continue to research and specify support policies that give more priorities to WSMEs, such as access to finance, governance, technology, and WSME incubation. Central and local organizations and associations could proactively seek and mobilize resources to accompany the government in the process of promoting policies to support WSMEs.

The White Book is fully supportive of initiatives to strengthen the business enabling environment for all SMEs. This includes progress on e-government, simplifying investment, land and tax procedures, and electronic customs clearance, shifting from pre-check (tiền kiểm) to post-check (hậu kiểm) investment procedures, and applying online systems for registering investment activities. Collecting data on gendered impact remains important, but targeting WSMEs for additional and special support is typically not justified.

The next section provides a summary analysis of the SME Support Law, leading to a recommendation for a comprehensive review of SME Support Law implementation. This is followed by details on the five action areas listed.

Vietnamese Small and Medium-Sized Enterprise Law: Moving from Intentions to Impacts

Chapter 5 noted limitations of the SME Support Law implementation and its rollout to the provinces. This section summarizes the ongoing challenges to implementing the law and offers recommendations.

The SME Support Law specification of access to credit and credit guarantee schemes, as elsewhere, lacks a gender lens. Such a lens might include requiring financial institutions to include WSME data in regular reports or funding pilot testing of new lending instruments for WSMEs (e.g., unsecured loan models). WSMEs are mentioned in a few sections of the law and its guiding documents but could certainly be more explicitly integrated into the variety of schemes. For example, Article 13, item 2 of Decree No. 80/2021/ND-CP dated 26 August 2021, specifies levels of support for micro, small, and medium enterprises in general, and WSMEs in particular.

The SME Support Law has many good intentions, including "supporting SMEs to develop feasible production and business plans, strengthen their governance capacity, management skills, and financial transparency to improve access to credit" (Article 8, Clause 2, Law on Support for SMEs); "providing incentives for credit institutions lending to SMEs with unsecured loans"; and establishing a Credit Guarantee Fund. The law also includes promises for "Exemption and reduction of corporate income taxes for a definite period in accordance with the law on corporate income tax for incubators, technical facilities, and co-working spaces (Article 12, Clause 3, Item b, Law on Supporting SMEs)."

In all these cases, however, the legal documents guiding implementation have no specific regulations on content. Furthermore, despite the policy being issued, its implementation at the provincial level is limited. As explained in Section 4.2.2, at the provincial level, quite a few SME Support Law initiatives have been undertaken, including in Thua Thien Hue Province and Can Tho city, where the Provincial People's Councils have issued resolutions stipulating support to SMEs in terms of rates for rental space in industrial parks. But overall progress has been slow and, most importantly, all these initiatives lack funding to support SMEs and, in practice, will never be able to satisfy demand from Viet Nam's 523,124 operating SMEs. In addition, the regulations on selecting SMEs for support have not been specified in detail, which results in limited access to the support policies. One of the main issues affecting the implementation of the SME support policies is the lack of guidance from the financial sector when the circular guiding the use of the state budget has not been issued in a timely manner. Therefore, SMEs seldom have access to the policies of Decree No. 80/2021/ND-CP, except for training support. At the local level, most localities have not arranged sufficient human and financial resources to carry out SME support activities when most of these support tasks are assigned to the Business Registration Office, a specialized unit for business registration or business support center. Limited human resources and unavailable funding put a large burden on the agencies to manage the support programs.

Some provisions of the SME Support Law have not been synchronously revised or concretized in any legal document. For example, Article 13 states that (a) enterprises and organizations investing in and operating product distribution chains that involve at least 80% of SMEs supplying made-in-Viet Nam products are entitled to the following support: (i) exemption from or reduction of land rental, land-use levy, and non-agricultural land-use tax in accordance with the law; (ii) exemption from or reduction of enterprise income tax for a specified period of time in accordance with the Law on Enterprise Income Tax; and (b) micro- and small-sized enterprises shall be prioritized in contractor selection in accordance with the bidding law. It also states that small- and medium-sized enterprises may enjoy a tax rate lower than the ordinary tax rate applied to enterprises. This limits the spillover impact and effectiveness of the SME Support Law over the past five years.

It may be worth comprehensively reviewing the implementation of the SME Support Law. Such a review begins with an understanding that budgets will always be small relative to the needs of 523,124 Vietnamese SMEs. The review could be guided by the objective of helping SMEs become more competitive rather than reducing the competition that SMEs are facing (i.e., with price-distorting subsidies like lower interest rates, tax cuts, or positive discrimination). Another point of agreement might be that spending government funds could prioritize actions that have potential to impact all SMEs. And finally, of course, a review of the SME Support Law implementation should systematically integrate gender considerations and have a strong gender lens monitoring and evaluation system.

With these points in mind, there are two broad recommendations that a review could focus on:

(i) **Fund experiments to pilot test and demonstrate ideas to prove the business case to SMEs, financial institutions, and policymakers that something is worth doing and scaling up.** For example, the uptake of the current credit guarantee schemes remains low in Viet Nam due to (i) long approval processes; (ii) reluctance to accept government-backed guarantees; (iii) limited managerial and administration capacity related to document appraisal, inspection, and supervision; and (iv) low awareness of these programs among small companies. However, there is an opportunity for the government to restructure them to be in line with international best practices and, in consultation with commercial banks, to shape them into more efficient programs that can effectively support financial institutions and better work for SMEs, particularly WSMEs. The example from the Republic of Korea[63] shows that credit guarantee schemes can be used to

63   The KIBO Technology Rating System, developed in 2005 by the Korea Technology Credit Guarantee Fund, aimed to promote viable technology ventures without a sufficient past financial track record. Targeted companies include ventures with high growth and technological potential. The rating system assesses management capability, technological excellence, market potential, and commercialization and generates two rating grades: technology business grade (success potential) and risk grade (default risk). Source: ADB. 2022. *Financial Access of Women-owned small and Medium sized Enterprises in Viet Nam.* Manila. p. 48.

build a modern credit assessment infrastructure that enables assessment of nontraditional assets such as patents, technology, and royalties.

(ii)   **Overhaul the approach to training and capacity building to bring it into the internet, and now, the artificial intelligence age.** Encourage and phase in the use of electronic information and learning products, all linked to a funded e-marketing strategy (i.e., not just put information, modules, and videos out there, but invest to get SME managers to know about the sites). Collect, analyze, and report performance data on the e-products (e.g., how many WSMEs and men-owned SMEs did an online short course) and use that feedback to change and add new products in a demand-led manner.

Five Action Areas for Promoting Women-Owned Small and Medium-Sized Enterprises

Embed Gender in SME Legal Documents

Clear and valid reference to WSMEs and gender equality could be integrated into all legal and policy documents. As part of this, the Law on Promulgation of Legal Documents, 2015 could be amended to ensure that the principle of gender equality is mainstreamed into policy documents at both national and provincial levels.

Despite strong foundational support for WSMEs in documents like the National Gender Equality Strategy and Decision No. 939/QD-TTg, the targets and activities listed are not well integrated into other legal and policy documents. More must be done to mainstream gender equality into the legal framework and the decision-making process. This means more thouroughly assessing the implications of any proposed new or amended policy on WEE and gender equality. As a first step, all SME legal and policy documents must contain clear and valid reference to WSMEs, women entrepreneurs, and gender equality. A target to achieve this was set for 2020 under Objective 7 of the National Gender Equality Strategy: "by 2020, 100% of legal drafts will be determined as having contents related to gender equality, gender inequality or discrimination." Laws to be prioritized with amendments to reflect this include the Law on Gender Equality, 2006; the Law on Organization of National Assembly, 2014; the Law on Organization of Government, 2015; and the Law on Organization of Local Government, 2015.

There is a need for better coordination across ministries at both the local and the national levels to implement WSME-specific support measures. The practical application of WSME support is still limited due to the lack of synchronization between the legal system and the policies of the Party and the state. As a result, WSMEs face difficulties in accessing support and incentives for development.

Regarding the measurement of outcomes through gender-disaggregated data, MPI could lead on implementing a coordinated system to better measure business and population data differentiated by gender and establishing a comprehensive database on WSMEs in the process. This type of policy can be used as the basis for well-informed policy development and implementation. Clear and valid targets and measurable key performance indicators could be set so that disaggregated impacts on WSMEs can be adequately observed. Targets from the National Strategy for Gender Equality can be better integrated into other relevant policy and legal documents.

MPI would benefit from developing a result-based monitoring and evaluation system to continually measure the quality of consultancy services delivered to SMEs, particularly those delivered to WSMEs. This mission could be added to the decree level. MPI is well placed to be the focal point for building a comprehensive monitoring and evaluation system to be applied across the country. MPI could also develop guidelines and set specific targets for implementation, as well as receive feedback from localities, evaluate the effectiveness and impact of the policies, and make recommendations for adjustments where needed.

The government might consider a legal solution to ensure collection and reporting of gender data, something like that in Spain or the UK (Box 3), or Malaysia. It is currently difficult to assess the status, needs, and policy impacts on WSMEs because of an absence of data collected and differentiated by gender. Tax data, for example, disaggregated by gender could be used to better gauge tax burdens and compliance issues specific to WSMEs. This information is vital for policymakers, financial institutions, and business support organizations to assess the situation and develop appropriate, evidence-based responses, policies, and products. In the case of legislative support, gender-disaggregated targets and key performance indicators could nevertheless be specified to better monitor impacts on WSMEs compared to men-owned SMEs. This allows the potentially gendered outcomes of a law or policy to be better assessed.

Legal documents are full of good intentions to support women doing business. One path to getting better results for women is to promulgate implementing regulations and urge their implementation. But without detailed measurement of results, of change—of reality—it cannot be said what has been achieved or not, and what to do about that. Another path to results is to start with the data. Adding the gender dimension to the 2021 Economic Census has been invaluable for this White Book. As noted, the census is part of a proposed set of activities to measure women doing business.

In future, all relevant WSME data could be analyzed and brought together for a high-level event 10 months after completing each census. Analysis of "Progress of Women in Business" could be presented alongside "Progress of Women in Politics and Administration" (e.g., National Assembly quotas, etc.). Numbers are convincing and influential. If the next census reports, for example, that women are still just 20% of Vietnamese SME owners, then the search for solutions must be intensified.

Directly Support Women-Owned Small and Medium-Sized Enterprises to Grow

Expert advisory services linked to support groups and business networking could be supported. A funded network of consultants to support WSMEs (in terms of technology, market, governance, trade promotion, and export and legal issues) can work with and through women entrepreneur's associations and women's business associations. One-stop-shops could facilitate WSME access to this consultancy support.

The provincial DPIs could cooperate with the Association of Enterprises, Women's Union, and other women business associations to hold training courses to disseminate knowledge to WSMEs on new changes to relevant laws and policies and how they can be of benefit to their business. Promoting policies and laws plays an important role in raising awareness within WSMEs about their legitimate rights and benefits, especially those in remote and isolated areas.

To grow, women-led household businesses must be encouraged to become formal enterprises. Household businesses, however, generally do not want to transform due to high corporate tax rates, increased accounting and financial compliance, the need for labor contracts, and more frequent inspections.

Aside from these transition challenges, it must be noted that most household businesses are not interested in growing. For them, the household business is a regular income, nothing more. Some, however, have the ambition to grow but are scared of becoming formalized and lack skills. Others have an ambition to grow, and perhaps even the skills, but over estimate the costs of being a formally established enterprise.

MPI could review its present package of assistance to encourage and "tip" households into becoming enterprises. A package might include funding tax consulting services for households to understand and meet the new requirements. Local People's Committees or Local People's Councils could help households to complete the registration process and explain tax incentives (for the first two years) to interested households. Access to free training and consulting services (e.g., business plans, human resource management, marketing plans, and access to finance help) can be conditional on having just become a formal enterprise. The Association of Enterprises and Women's Unions could deliver such assistance.

The process of becoming a formal enterprise could be reviewed and further simplified, as has been done through the MyCOID System in Malaysia and the BizFile System in Singapore. The number of application documents can be reduced. For example, only a signed incorporation form may be necessary, without requiring a list of shareholders and a company charter. The required documents could be limited to a business household registration certificate, tax code registration certificate, and one signed registration form. Electronic versions of the Enterprise Registration Certificate could be permitted for doing business, and registration fees are abolished.

An awareness-raising campaign would complement these initiatives and reduce misinformation and uncertainty among households about the actual costs and benefits of becoming an enterprise. Integral to such a campaign is the promotion of role model WSME success stories.

Strengthen Women-Owned Small and Medium-Sized Enterprise Capacities and Knowledge

Develop an ecosystem (business clubs) to support and partner with women entrepreneurs, especially networks of successful local entrepreneurs to provide mentorship for WSMEs. SMEs, in particular WSMEs, will benefit greatly from more relevant information and knowledge. To be most effective, however, such activities could be linked to and strengthen business networks. Business clubs under the Women's Union or other organizations can foster group mentorship through business tours, events, and e-learning. Blended training and consultancy and mixing online training and on-site consultancy for WSMEs is a cost-effective approach. Government agencies could study and consider implementing a model similar to the Australian leadership community and networking service, CUB.

More basic knowledge dissemination activities are needed to make WSMEs better aware of business processes and existing policy support measures. This might include advertising campaigns, training, and e-resources. An example is Malaysia's eKelas Usahawan program. The White Book research found that a lack of knowledge and understanding about policy support mechanisms and general business processes remains a significant barrier facing WSMEs in Viet Nam. This includes guidance about electronic tax declarations, business registration, and preferential schemes for tax relief and loans. Many WSMEs are not aware of existing support mechanisms and miss opportunities for greater engagement with both state and professional and social organizations assistance. Greater information sharing through local professional and social organizations and interactive web pages (or an app) will help address this knowledge gap. Such knowledge products then become learning tools for physical gatherings of WSME business clubs, one-stop-shops for government services, provincial information portals, and others. Basic knowledge dissemination activities include efforts to make WSMEs more aware of existing resources, such as the credit-connection portal/app "CIC Credit Connect (Kết nối nhu cầu vay)" (available in Vietnamese).

Government agencies could adopt a more "customer-focused" philosophy and more effective information services to support WSMEs. Tax departments, for example, could provide in-person guidance for WSMEs and SMEs about tax declarations and payments. MPI could enhance the attractiveness and usefulness of the National SME Support Portal, including links with other national and provincial SME websites and business support ecosystem actors, to make the portal a genuine learning and information hub for WSMEs. This would include integrating the National SME Support Portal with available digital tools for WSME capacity building, such as the SME E-Learning Platform, Credit-Connection Portal of the the National Credit Information Center of Viet Nam (CIC), and SME Capacity Assessment Diagnostic toolkits.

Central and provincial government agencies could work in partnership with Unions, credit agencies, business support organizations, and professional and social organizations to deliver a coordinated system of business skills training for women entrepreneurs. WSMEs in Viet Nam suffer from a lack of skills regarding business administration, accounting, management, and marketing. This is felt by women business owners but is also reflected in the view of Women's Unions and credit agencies. Targeted and inclusive training in partnership with existing professional and social organizations (and using e-learning tools) can help address these skill shortfalls. In addition, central and provincial government agencies could work in partnership with Unions, credit agencies, business support organizations, and professional and social organizations to further develop one-on-one coaching, which is effective and preferred by a number of women entrepreneurs because of its practicality. However, it requires a very good matchmaker who understands mentors and mentees and genuine effort from mentees.

Developing and delivering highly relevant e-learning products (often with blended delivery that builds networks) would benefit from economies of scale (i.e., be relevant to all provinces). Currently, there are examples of such training taking place in some provinces but without central-level coordination. As such, training is uncoordinated and of mixed quality.

The curriculum of training products and services should be adjusted regularly based on evaluations and critical feedback from participants. The e-learning products should build on what has already been done and put existing useful materials on e-Learning platforms (including curricula of the Ministry of Industry and Trade (MOIT) for exporters about product design development, quality control, and product promotion abroad).

All curricula should incorporate a gender lens, which includes consideration of the specific needs of women doing business and addressing the psychological and social obstacles faced by women.

Strengthen Women-Owned Small and Medium-Sized Enterprise Access to Finance

Develop an "access to finance" WSME-focused action plan to incentivize and facilitate greater engagement with women entrepreneurs from the commercial banking sector. Women entrepreneurs still struggle to access finance. In part, this is due to a lack of awareness of financing opportunities, alongside uncertainties around application processes and financial management. This awareness problem is the consequence of the underlying problem of WSMEs being smaller and less ambitious than the average men-owned SME, again reflecting societal norms. Mobilizing support from the commercial banking sector, such as sponsoring networking events and tailored products, will encourage better engagement with women entrepreneurs. An action plan would also assist interested WSMEs to develop more comprehensive business and financial plans, guide them through the loan appraisal process, and provide what they need to achieve a strong credit rating. This should target households that recently became enterprises, as a typical main reason for the transition was to gain access to formal sources of finance.

Encourage financial institutions to develop focused products, such as loans with pledges on future receivables or leasing. Banks and other financial institutions should be encouraged to develop products that offer more flexibility, including softer collateral requirements. This will facilitate gender-conscious interventions, which includes collecting gender-disaggregated data at the portfolio level on a regular basis and using this to design and implement gender-sensitive bank strategies, and develop products and services better tailored to the specific needs and preferences of women-owned businesses. This could be done by mandating the collection of gender-disaggregated data by law, as in Malaysia or Spain, or by encouraging financial institutions to sign up voluntarily and pledge to do so as in the UK.

Undertake Activities Targeting Changes in Societal Norms and Values

A women's empowerment ambassador program could be established to showcase the value of WEE and to promote and champion women's entrepreneurship. As with examples from Sweden, this could be a publicly funded program and emphasize diversity of ethnicity, age, industry, company size, and geographic region. Gendered behavioral norms and learned behaviors still pose a major foundational barrier to gender equality and the development of women's entrepreneurship. An ambassador program works to increase the visibility of women entrepreneurship and can inspire Vietnamese women through personal stories and role models. The example of the women's ambassador program in Sweden could be adopted by the Women's Union. Such a program helps challenge internalized gender norms and promote gender equality and can be linked to engagement with leaders, agencies, and departments in charge of implementing policy.

Government ministries could lead on gender norms training among civil servants at national and provincial levels. Gender norms and learned behaviors still pose a major foundational barrier to gender equality and the development of women's entrepreneurship. More could be done to spread awareness and understanding of these barriers through knowledge sharing and training. National and provincial government officials could all receive gender norms training in partnership with professional and social organizations. An emphasis should be placed on engaging with men and boys. Such training would promote gender awareness and gender equality mainstreaming in all policymaking and implementation at both national and provincial levels.

APPENDIX 1
SME and WSME Definitions

For the purpose of clarification, the report defines a small and medium-sized enterprise (SME) as per Table A1. This definition follows the definition set out by the 2017 Law on Supporting SMEs.

Women-owned small and medium-sized enterprises are defined by the SME Support Law as SMEs with (i) at least 51% of their charter capital owned by one or more women and (ii) at least a woman as a manager or executive director of this enterprise.

Table A1: Legal Definition of Micro, Small, and Medium-Sized Enterprises

Criteria	Micro	Small	Medium
Annual revenue	Legal definition: ≤ D10 billion ($0.43 million)[a] in commerce and services ≤ D3 billion ($0.13 million) in agriculture, forestry, and aquaculture; and industry and construction	Legal definition: ≤ D100 billion ($4.3 million) in commerce and services ≤ D50 ($2.1 million) billion in agriculture, forestry, and aquaculture; and industry and construction	Legal definition: ≤ D300 billion ($12.8 million) in commerce and services ≤ D200 billion ($8.5 million) in agriculture, forestry, and aquaculture; and industry and construction
Total capital/ total assets	Legal definition: ≤ D3 billion ($0.13 million)	Legal definition: ≤ D50 billion ($2.1 million) in commerce and services ≤ D20 billion ($0.85 million) in agriculture, forestry, aquaculture, and industry and construction	Legal definition: ≤ D100 billion ($4.3 million) in commerce and services agriculture, forestry, and aquaculture; and industry and construction
Total employees	Legal definition: ≤ 10 employees	Legal definition: ≤ 50 employees in commerce and services ≤ 100 employees in agriculture, forestry, aquaculture, and industry and construction	Legal definition: ≤ 100 employees in commerce and services ≤ 200 employees in agriculture, forestry, aquaculture, and industry and construction

D = Viet Nam dong.

[a] As per Article 5, Decree No. 80/2021/ND-CP dated 26 August 2021 guiding the SME Support Law, the micro, small, and medium enterprise definition is based on the average annual number of employees participating in social insurance, and total revenue or total capital.

Source: Government of Viet Nam Decree No. 80/2021/ND-CP dated 26 August 2021 on elaboration of some articles of the Law on SME Support, Article 5.

APPENDIX 2
Methodology

The White Book extensively uses data from the unprecedented 2021 Economic Census, which covered all 63 provinces and cities nationwide and analyzed the women-owned small and medium-sized enterprise (WSME) dataset. With support from We-Fi and the Asian Development Bank (ADB) and technical guidance provided by the Agency for Enterprise Development (Ministry of Planning and Investment) under this project, this was the first time WSME data was collected nationwide about each WSME. Questionnaire 1.15 (Q1.15) was included in this census to ask about WSMEs only.

Five questions were integrated into the questionnaires of the 2021 Economic Census (Q1.15) to collect additional information to accurately identify WSMEs, focusing on

- number of employees having social insurance;
- the enterprise's total capital or revenue of the previous year;
- number of women among the owners of the enterprise;
- the percentage of the enterprise's charter capital owned by women; and
- is there a woman top manager among the owners of the enterprise?

In addition, a set of 20 questions focusing on the following information was also included in the census to gain a better understanding of the characteristics and performance of the WSMEs as well as monitor the support activities for WSMEs under the SME Support Law (Q1.15):

- loans for business and production;
- ability to expand the market and participate in the supply chain of products, the industry cluster, and value chain;
- WSMEs transformed into enterprises from business households;
- training program to improve the quality of human resources;
- brand development activities;
- innovations;
- digital transformation;
- state supports received in connection with the above activities.

Additionally, this study incorporates findings from further surveys, interviews, consultations with stakeholders, policy and regulatory framework reviews, and a barrier study. The primary data collection was conducted from August 2021 to April 2022, and comprises the following components.

Component on the Policy and Legal Review and Barrier Study

Stakeholder consultations and interviews were held with government agencies, Vietnamese Women's Unions, business networks, entrepreneurship associations, and WSME owners and representatives at both central and provincial levels.

At the central level, the team conducted interviews with the following agencies and organizations:

- Enterprise Development Agency, Ministry of Planning and Investment;
- Small and Medium Enterprise Development Fund (SMEDF);
- National Credit Information Center (CIC), State Bank of Viet Nam;
- Department of Tax Policy, Ministry of Finance;
- Directorate of Vocational Education and Training, Ministry of Labour, Invalids and Social Affairs;
- Trade Promotion Agency and Agency for Regional Industry and Trade, Ministry of Industry and Trade;
- Department of International Relations and Department of Civil Code, Ministry of Justice
- Women's Union;
- Viet Nam SME Association (VINASME)
- Women's Association of Vietnamese Entrepreneurs (WAVE)

At the provincial level, the team conducted in-depth interviews with the following agencies and organizations in four provinces (Lam Dong, Thua Thien Hue, Can Tho, and Lao Cai) with the Department of Planning and Investment, Department of Finance, Department of Tax, Department of Justice, Department of Science and Technology, Department of Information and Communication, provincial branches of State Bank, credit guarantee funds, provincial Women's Unions, provincial women business associations, provincial business associations, and 10 WSMEs in each province.

A survey was conducted with WSMEs focusing on the broader barriers to women's entrepreneurship, including information on the legal framework, and impact of the COVID-19 pandemic on their businesses. Due to budget constraints and the pandemic context, a small survey with 118 WSME women owners was completed.[1]

---

[1]   The survey was conducted late 2021 to early 2022 when travel restrictions were still in place in Viet Nam due to the pandemic.

Component on Access to Finance

- The project team administered an "access to finance" focused questionnaire-based survey with a sample size of 304 SMEs. The project team administered a questionnaire survey to 36 banks, with support from the SBV. In total, 27 institutions contributed to the study, including Agribank, VietinBank, Vietcombank, and BIDV.

The survey was supplemented with data collected through in-depth interviews with 55 WSMEs. A total of 10 banks were interviewed to complement data collected through the survey and capture their experience serving women-owned businesses. Key informant interviews were done with other sector stakeholders, including representatives from four departments of the State Bank of Viet Nam (Monetary Policy Department, Credit Department, Statistics and Forecast Department, and Banking Strategy Institute), MoF, two associations (VINASME and Viet Nam Women Entrepreneurs Council), and credit guarantee funds.

APPENDIX 3

Innovating Women-Owned Small and Medium-Sized Enterprises in Thua Thien Hue Province

Table A3.1: Innovating Women-Owned Small and Medium-Sized Enterprises

Item	Number of WSMEs (Q 1.15)	Having Activities to Innovate, Improve Products, Services, Processes, and Business Models		WSMEs Implementing Innovation Activities Who Got at least One Type of State Support (Number)	WSMEs Implementing Innovation Activities Who Got at least One Type of State Support (%)
		WSMEs (Number)	WSMEs (%)		
All WSMEs	**110,667**	**13,040**	**12**	**2,511**	**19**
Northern Central area and Central Coastal area	14,630	1,608	11	384	24
Thua Thien Hue	662	91	14	22	24

WSMEs = women-owned small and medium-sized enterprises.
Source: GSO. 2021. Economic Census.

Table A3.2: Women-Owned Small and Medium-Sized Enterprises Implementing Innovation Activities by State Support Received

Item	Number of WSMEs (Q1.15)	Total	Consulting on Intellectual Property, Exploitation, and Development of Intellectual Property	Support Procedures on Standards, Technical Regulations, Perfecting New Products, New Business Models	Support for Technology Application and Transfer	Support for Training, Information, and Trade Promotion of Technology Products and Services	Support Using Technical Facilities, Incubators, and Co-working Areas	Supporting Preferential Credit Capital to Implement Innovation Activities	Other
All WSMEs	**110,667**	**3,620**	**619**	**868**	**514**	**908**	**185**	**478**	**48**
Northern Central area and Central Coastal area	14,630	552	75	131	72	134	27	105	8
Thua Thien Hue	662	31	8	9	4	9	0	1	0

WSMEs = women-owned small and medium-sized enterprises.
Source: General Statistics Office. 2021. Economic Census.

APPENDIX 4
Additional Data Tables about WSMEs in Viet Nam

Table A4.1: Women-Owned Small and Medium-Sized Enterprises
Operating as of 31 December 2020 by Size and Province

Province	Number of SMEs	WSMEs (Number)				WSMEs (%)			
		Micro	Small	Medium	Total	Micro	Small	Medium	Total
Whole country	**523,124**	**72,874**	**29,425**	**3,577**	**105,876**	**69**	**28**	**3**	**100**
Northern Midlands and Mountain areas	**22,661**	**2,248**	**1,477**	**159**	**3,884**	**58**	**38**	**4**	**100**
Ha Giang	725	51	38	6	95	54	40	6	100
Cao Bang	793	97	57	6	160	61	36	4	100
Bac Kan	446	45	20	–	65	69	31	0	100
Tuyen Quang	1,020	117	62	2	181	65	34	1	100
Lao Cai	1,729	213	127	23	363	59	35	6	100
Dien Bien	747	100	77	5	182	55	42	3	100
Lai Chau	662	51	48	2	101	50	48	2	100
Son La	1,406	132	70	13	215	61	33	6	100
Yen Bai	1,132	128	76	5	209	61	36	2	100
Hoa Binh	1,440	138	87	9	234	59	37	4	100
Thai Nguyen	3,270	310	208	22	540	57	39	4	100
Lang Son	1,402	175	147	18	340	51	43	5	100
Bac Giang	4,199	357	246	32	635	56	39	5	100
Phu Tho	3,690	334	214	16	564	59	38	3	100
Red River Delta	**168,335**	**20,426**	**9,401**	**1,230**	**31,057**	**66**	**30**	**4**	**100**
Ha Noi	110,795	14,537	5,819	704	21,060	69	28	3	100
Quang Ninh	5,873	726	423	35	1,184	61	36	3	100
Vinh Phuc	4,944	479	240	33	752	64	32	4	100
Bac Ninh	8,565	987	610	106	1,703	58	36	6	100
Hai Duong	6,295	575	361	58	994	58	36	6	100

continued on next page

Table A4.1 *continued*

Province	Number of SMEs	WSMEs (Number)				WSMEs (%)			
		Micro	Small	Medium	Total	Micro	Small	Medium	Total
Hai Phong	12,924	1,496	866	98	2,460	61	35	4	100
Hung Yen	4,947	438	260	57	755	58	34	8	100
Thai Binh	3,434	318	193	34	545	58	35	6	100
Ha Nam	3,047	218	184	32	434	50	42	7	100
Nam Dinh	4,495	402	256	42	700	57	37	6	100
Ninh Binh	3,016	250	189	31	470	53	40	7	100
Northern Central area and Central Coastal area	**71,865**	**9,949**	**3,414**	**342**	**13,705**	**73**	**25**	**2**	**100**
Thanh Hoa	7,985	810	367	57	1,234	66	30	5	100
Nghe An	8,238	622	296	22	940	66	31	2	100
Ha Tinh	3,219	293	136	9	438	67	31	2	100
Quang Binh	3,042	373	123	2	498	75	25	0	100
Quang Tri	1,992	320	142	12	474	68	30	3	100
Thua Thien Hue	3,325	437	167	12	616	71	27	2	100
Da Nang	16,337	3,237	768	71	4,076	79	19	2	100
Quang Nam	5,345	679	210	17	906	75	23	2	100
Quang Ngai	3,783	504	185	19	708	71	26	3	100
Binh Dinh	5,047	676	319	45	1,040	65	31	4	100
Phu Yen	2,043	330	104	15	449	73	23	3	100
Khanh Hoa	6,656	1,097	339	32	1,468	75	23	2	100
Ninh Thuan	1,744	179	107	10	296	60	36	3	100
Binh Thuan	3,109	392	151	19	562	70	27	3	100
Central Highlands	**14,238**	**2,159**	**893**	**74**	**3,126**	**69**	**29**	**2**	**100**
Kon Tum	1,126	171	85	8	264	65	32	3	100
Gia Lai	2,920	387	177	19	583	66	30	3	100
Dak Lak	4,534	620	256	21	897	69	29	2	100
Dak Nong	1,464	241	121	6	368	65	33	2	100
Lam Dong	4,194	740	254	20	1,014	73	25	2	100
South East	**204,079**	**32,173**	**11,709**	**1,455**	**45,337**	**71**	**26**	**3**	**100**
Binh Phuoc	3,346	446	254	58	758	59	34	8	100
Tay Ninh	2,859	417	183	26	626	67	29	4	100
Binh Duong	22,122	2,715	1,559	237	4,511	60	35	5	100
Dong Nai	15,738	1,843	971	126	2,940	63	33	4	100
Ba Ria – Vung Tau	7,096	1,011	399	42	1,452	70	27	3	100

continued on next page

Table A4.1 *continued*

Province	Number of SMEs	WSMEs (Number)				WSMEs (%)			
		Micro	Small	Medium	Total	Micro	Small	Medium	Total
Ho Chi Minh	152,918	25,741	8,343	966	35,050	73	24	3	100
Mekong River Delta	**41,926**	**5,919**	**2,531**	**317**	**8,767**	**68**	**29**	**4**	**100**
Long An	6,606	724	444	100	1,268	57	35	8	100
Tien Giang	3,724	625	272	27	924	68	29	3	100
Ben Tre	2,477	338	172	15	525	64	33	3	100
Tra Vinh	1,591	220	76	10	306	72	25	3	100
Vinh Long	1,945	286	120	8	414	69	29	2	100
Dong Thap	2,749	447	166	22	635	70	26	3	100
An Giang	3,339	488	231	16	735	66	31	2	100
Kien Giang	5,272	844	311	26	1,181	71	26	2	100
Can Tho	6,463	832	254	32	1,118	74	23	3	100
Hau Giang	1,435	218	103	11	332	66	31	3	100
Soc Trang	2,104	257	91	15	363	71	25	4	100
Bac Lieu	1,592	226	106	17	349	65	30	5	100
Ca Mau	2,629	414	185	18	617	67	30	3	100
No partion	20								

SMEs = small and medium-sized enterprises, WSMEs = women-owned small and medium-sized enterprises.
Source: General Statistics Office. 2021. Economic Census.

Table A4.2: Women-Owned Small and Medium-Sized Enterprises Operating as of 31 December 2020 by Size and Economic Sector

Economic Sector	SMEs (Number)	WSMEs (Number)				WSMEs (%)			
		Micro	Small	Medium	Total	Micro	Small	Medium	Total
Whole country	**523,124**	**72,874**	**29,425**	**3,577**	**105,876**	**69**	**28**	**3**	**100**
Agriculture, forestry, and fishing	4,121	329	322	22	**673**	49	48	3	**100**
Mining and quarrying	2,239	102	143	22	**267**	38	54	8	**100**
Manufacturing	81,602	7,324	6,048	1,094	**14,466**	51	42	8	**100**
Electricity, gas, stream, and air conditioning supply	3,250	416	95	26	**537**	77	18	5	**100**
Water supply, sewerage, waste management, and remediation activities	2,043	229	94	8	**331**	69	28	2	**100**
Construction	71,747	3,590	3,138	371	**7,099**	51	44	5	**100**
Wholesale and retail trade; repair of motor vehicles and motorcycles	204,271	34,456	13,244	1,355	**49,055**	70	27	3	**100**
Transportation and storage	31,986	4,824	1,777	151	**6,752**	71	26	2	**100**
Accommodation and food service activities	19,142	4,995	906	76	**5,977**	84	15	1	**100**
Information and communication	11,030	1,249	277	36	**1,562**	80	18	2	**100**
Financial, banking, and insurance activities	2,240	480	141	11	**632**	76	22	2	**100**
Real estate activities	11,655	1,735	493	68	**2,296**	76	21	3	**100**
Professional, scientific, and technical activities	43,578	6,031	1,058	68	**7,157**	84	15	1	**100**
Administrative and support service activities	20,312	3,966	766	110	**4,842**	82	16	2	**100**
Education and training	6,127	1,632	561	90	**2,283**	71	25	4	**100**
Human health and social work activities	2,109	301	195	44	**540**	56	36	8	**100**
Arts, entertainment, and recreation	2,247	442	73	15	**530**	83	14	3	**100**
Other service activities	3,425	773	94	10	**877**	88	11	1	**100**

SMEs = small and medium-sized enterprises, WSMEs = women-owned small and medium-sized enterprises.

Source: General Statistics Office. 2021. Economic Census.

Table A4.3: Average Number of Employees per Women-Owned Small and Medium-Sized Enterprise Operating as of 31 December 2020 by Province

Province	SME	WSME			
		Micro	Small	Medium	Total
Whole country	**9**	**3**	**14**	**49**	**8**
Northern Midlands and Mountain areas	**15**	**4**	**16**	**58**	**11**
Ha Giang	23	5	19	124	18
Cao Bang	18	4	17	93	12
Bac Kan	11	3	20		8
Tuyen Quang	16	4	18	84	10
Lao Cai	14	4	15	38	10
Dien Bien	19	4	19	106	13
Lai Chau	10	4	10	36	8
Son La	9	4	11	31	8
Yen Bai	18	4	19	99	12
Hoa Binh	14	4	16	54	10
Thai Nguyen	13	4	15	34	10
Lang Son	12	4	9	36	8
Bac Giang	15	4	18	76	13
Phu Tho	15	4	18	69	11
Red River Delta	**10**	**4**	**14**	**47**	**8**
Ha Noi	9	3	13	41	7
Quang Ninh	12	4	13	57	9
Vinh Phuc	12	4	16	60	10
Bac Ninh	14	3	13	32	9
Hai Duong	15	4	18	69	13
Hai Phong	11	4	14	49	9
Hung Yen	14	4	17	71	13
Thai Binh	17	4	22	72	15
Ha Nam	15	3	16	63	13
Nam Dinh	13	4	16	55	11
Ninh Binh	14	4	17	53	12
Northern Central area and Central Coastal area	**10**	**4**	**16**	**59**	**8**
Thanh Hoa	12	4	17	63	11
Nghe An	12	4	18	59	10
Ha Tinh	13	4	18	69	10
Quang Binh	10	4	15	39	7
Quang Tri	9	4	13	28	7
Thua Thien Hue	11	4	15	65	8

continued on next page

Table A4.3 *continued*

Province	SME	WSME			
		Micro	Small	Medium	Total
Da Nang	8	3	16	54	7
Quang Nam	10	4	18	67	8
Quang Ngai	9	3	16	59	8
Binh Dinh	14	4	19	65	11
Phu Yen	11	4	18	83	10
Khanh Hoa	11	3	16	54	7
Ninh Thuan	8	3	13	48	8
Binh Thuan	9	3	15	56	8
Central Highlands	**9**	**3**	**12**	**49**	**7**
Kon Tum	12	4	16	74	10
Gia Lai	10	3	14	50	8
Dak Lak	9	3	13	52	7
Dak Nong	7	3	6	29	5
Lam Dong	8	3	11	39	6
South East	**8**	**3**	**12**	**48**	**7**
Binh Phuoc	10	4	13	25	8
Tay Ninh	12	3	14	52	9
Binh Duong	12	3	14	67	10
Dong Nai	10	3	13	55	9
Ba Ria – Vung Tau	9	3	13	65	8
Ho Chi Minh	7	3	12	43	6
Mekong River Delta	**10**	**4**	**16**	**53**	**9**
Long An	14	3	17	56	12
Tien Giang	11	3	21	72	10
Ben Tre	11	4	21	66	11
Tra Vinh	8	4	13	82	9
Vinh Long	10	4	20	39	9
Dong Thap	8	4	14	37	7
An Giang	7	4	11	38	7
Kien Giang	9	4	16	51	8
Can Tho	7	4	13	41	7
Hau Giang	8	4	13	40	8
Soc Trang	9	4	17	30	8
Bac Lieu	10	4	15	80	11
Ca Mau	9	4	13	39	8

SMEs = small and medium-sized enterprises, WSMEs = women-owned small and medium-sized enterprises.
Source: General Statistics Office. 2021. Economic Census.

Table A4.4: Average Number of Employees per Women-Owned Small and Medium-Sized Enterprise Operating as of 31 December 2020 by Economic Sector

Economic Sector	SME	WSME			
		Micro	Small	Medium	Total
Whole country	9	3	14	49	8
Agriculture, forestry, and fishing	16	4	21	52	13
Mining and quarrying	18	4	17	50	15
Manufacturing	18	3	19	69	15
Electricity, gas, stream, and air conditioning supply	8	3	11	27	5
Water supply, sewerage, waste management, and remediation activities	15	3	17	65	9
Construction	13	3	15	55	11
Wholesale and retail trade; repair of motor vehicles and motorcycles	6	3	10	27	5
Transportation and storage	9	4	14	50	7
Accommodation and food service activities	8	4	18	67	6
Information and communication	10	3	18	58	7
Financial, banking, and insurance activities	9	4	16	63	8
Real estate activities	8	3	14	45	7
Professional, scientific, and technical activities	7	3	16	62	6
Administrative and support service activities	8	3	18	65	7
Education and training	11	4	23	68	11
Human health and social work activities	18	4	25	68	17
Arts, entertainment, and recreation	8	3	18	66	7
Other service activities	6	3	21	67	6

SME = small and medium-sized enterprise, WSME = women-owned small and medium-sized enterprise.
Source: General Statistics Office. 2021. Economic Census.

Table A4.5: Key Indicators of Women-Owned Small and Medium-Sized Enterprises Operating as of 31 December 2020 by Province
(D million)

Province	Avg. Owners' Equity		Avg. Fixed Assets		Avg. Net Turnover		Avg. Pre-tax Profit		Avg. After Tax Profit		Payable per Employee		Contribution to Trade Union, Social Insurance, Health Insurance, Unemployment Insurance per Employee	
	Per SME	Per WSME	Per SME	Per WSME	Per SME	Per WSME	Per SME	Per WSME	Per SME	Per WSME	SMEs	WSMEs	SMEs	WSMEs
Whole country	**9,397**	**6,373**	**2,908**	**1,805**	**13,374**	**12,986**	**(13)**	**(45)**	**(48)**	**(66)**	**91**	**81**	**16**	**8**
Northern Midlands and Mountain areas	**10,033**	**6,668**	**5,872**	**3,436**	**15,313**	**15,722**	**(40)**	**(32)**	**(62)**	**(40)**	**80**	**71**	**7**	**6**
Ha Giang	16,263	5,622	16,236	3,995	14,750	11,378	(45)	78	(97)	54	66	59	4	2
Cao Bang	8,544	5,655	6,319	3,128	13,080	11,422	65	126	30	98	84	69	4	4
Bac Kan	9,425	6,092	5,092	2,187	9,258	5,029	(196)	(130)	(206)	(135)	91	63	6	4
Tuyen Quang	6,115	4,354	2,305	1,150	13,392	7,606	173	22	150	14	94	61	6	5
Lao Cai	14,547	12,848	8,193	9,417	17,246	17,616	260	114	235	98	90	85	5	5
Dien Bien	11,249	6,265	8,425	1,845	12,198	14,040	252	288	238	283	62	58	4	3
Lai Chau	16,663	11,325	9,071	3,602	13,225	16,232	166	75	159	72	78	65	6	4
Son La	15,463	9,051	11,132	9,250	14,621	19,751	356	473	329	468	72	64	8	7
Yen Bai	9,382	4,373	6,908	3,112	14,805	11,758	55	16	27	10	81	63	7	5
Hoa Binh	10,598	9,326	6,033	3,593	12,144	12,412	(169)	46	(188)	38	72	70	7	6
Thai Nguyen	8,285	7,117	4,251	1,748	18,653	19,811	(195)	(228)	(215)	(233)	87	74	8	7
Lang Son	8,361	5,419	3,578	2,414	20,770	26,783	(260)	(201)	(270)	(207)	73	68	7	7
Bac Giang	10,249	4,992	4,266	2,120	14,903	13,937	(166)	(264)	(189)	(270)	86	81	9	7
Phu Tho	6,586	4,307	4,395	2,492	14,352	13,476	(106)	(10)	(121)	(17)	75	70	6	5
Red River Delta	**10,543**	**7,600**	**2,674**	**1,709**	**14,390**	**14,231**	**11**	**(50)**	**(22)**	**(68)**	**93**	**84**	**29**	**8**
Ha Noi	10,865	7,761	1,839	1,327	12,816	12,554	31	(34)	(3)	(52)	99	89	46	9

continued on next page

Table A4.5 continued

Province	Avg. Owners' Equity		Avg. Fixed Assets		Avg. Net Turnover		Avg. Pre-tax Profit		Avg. After Tax Profit		Payable per Employee		Contribution to Trade Union, Social Insurance, Health Insurance, Unemployment Insurance per Employee	
	Per SME	Per WSME	Per SME	Per WSME	Per SME	Per WSME	Per SME	Per WSME	Per SME	Per WSME	SMEs	WSMEs	SMEs	WSMEs
Quang Ninh	12,698	6,268	5,067	2,801	16,481	14,715	87	(129)	59	(144)	82	78	8	7
Vinh Phuc	11,004	11,657	3,669	1,858	13,814	14,338	(98)	(82)	(120)	(95)	88	76	8	6
Bac Ninh	10,785	7,619	4,095	2,044	20,527	20,320	167	101	106	67	107	88	9	5
Hai Duong	7,813	4,769	3,656	2,095	14,778	14,679	(55)	(169)	(80)	(179)	85	77	8	7
Hai Phong	8,210	5,119	3,679	2,038	18,882	18,589	(50)	(35)	(80)	(54)	90	80	9	8
Hung Yen	10,960	9,036	5,198	3,243	18,928	18,877	44	(213)	10	(230)	92	84	9	7
Thai Binh	9,558	7,281	4,129	2,930	13,653	14,821	(295)	(331)	(308)	(339)	68	66	4	3
Ha Nam	12,607	13,874	6,514	4,517	19,395	21,468	(184)	(183)	(214)	(198)	84	76	8	7
Nam Dinh	8,724	6,108	4,477	2,729	16,601	18,793	(67)	(70)	(81)	(79)	64	61	4	3
Ninh Binh	9,827	10,611	4,284	4,115	16,643	20,544	(135)	(125)	(144)	(128)	71	63	5	5
Northern Central area and Central Coastal area	**7,557**	**4,728**	**4,137**	**2,422**	**10,138**	**9,666**	**(204)**	**(95)**	**(225)**	**(106)**	**71**	**62**	**6**	**5**
Thanh Hoa	9,109	6,675	3,369	3,155	11,083	12,760	(26)	(90)	(37)	(98)	67	62	4	4
Nghe An	7,090	5,166	4,013	2,303	10,549	12,333	(37)	(86)	(55)	(95)	68	60	6	6
Ha Tinh	8,118	5,215	3,769	2,972	9,952	9,225	58	(38)	46	(44)	74	66	5	5
Quang Binh	8,584	7,054	4,531	2,825	9,755	7,282	(257)	(152)	(263)	(154)	64	46	6	5
Quang Tri	6,999	4,623	5,661	4,105	13,449	16,771	(76)	(174)	(89)	(178)	67	57	6	5
Thua Thien Hue	7,364	3,414	3,825	1,480	9,743	7,348	49	(79)	14	(88)	69	56	7	5
Da Nang	5,681	3,844	2,348	1,736	7,852	6,472	(182)	(169)	(205)	(178)	79	66	7	6

continued on next page

Table A4.5 *continued*

Province	Avg. Owners' Equity		Avg. Fixed Assets		Avg. Net Turnover		Avg. Pre-tax Profit		Avg. After Tax Profit		Payable per Employee		Contribution to Trade Union, Social Insurance, Health Insurance, Unemployment Insurance per Employee	
	Per SME	Per WSME	Per SME	Per WSME	Per SME	Per WSME	Per SME	Per WSME	Per SME	Per WSME	SMEs	WSMEs	SMEs	WSMEs
Quang Nam	7,330	3,725	3,818	2,238	7,528	6,216	(224)	(136)	(238)	(142)	70	65	6	6
Quang Ngai	6,056	4,971	3,032	1,323	10,466	11,399	(621)	(190)	(642)	(198)	77	66	5	4
Binh Dinh	7,448	6,003	4,089	3,194	13,934	15,309	98	17	59	(6)	71	66	4	3
Phu Yen	6,608	3,564	4,451	1,311	10,800	13,935	(7)	(68)	(18)	(76)	64	57	5	3
Khanh Hoa	9,511	4,223	5,559	3,243	10,398	7,842	(1,125)	208	(1,151)	191	71	59	6	5
Ninh Thuan	11,001	4,641	14,458	4,080	12,873	13,851	469	76	449	57	75	63	6	5
Binh Thuan	10,538	6,461	8,122	2,930	12,903	12,665	(284)	(468)	(306)	(484)	69	63	5	4
Central Highlands	**8,664**	**4,804**	**5,642**	**2,974**	**14,079**	**17,108**	**(5)**	**(153)**	**(21)**	**(161)**	**78**	**63**	**5**	**4**
Kon Tum	15,348	7,943	12,720	6,042	15,635	20,647	119	(86)	99	(94)	72	59	5	3
Gia Lai	12,297	6,437	6,283	3,619	14,428	17,676	(134)	(316)	(149)	(325)	71	70	4	3
Dak Lak	6,421	3,717	5,118	1,870	13,290	15,503	33	(166)	17	(172)	85	59	5	4
Dak Nong	8,367	3,570	6,554	1,513	19,482	24,051	102	(79)	90	(82)	73	63	7	3
Lam Dong	6,869	4,458	3,545	3,312	12,387	14,762	(26)	(93)	(44)	(101)	78	64	7	5
South East	**9,407**	**6,200**	**2,032**	**1,282**	**13,077**	**12,051**	**26**	**(19)**	**(18)**	**(46)**	**105**	**93**	**13**	**10**
Binh Phuoc	12,571	10,017	8,338	5,468	23,182	24,390	46	(22)	10	(33)	82	76	5	3
Tay Ninh	10,235	5,066	6,074	3,181	17,288	17,745	75	182	35	166	85	65	9	4
Binh Duong	9,816	5,567	3,584	2,030	16,503	15,203	98	9	44	(19)	98	89	12	10
Dong Nai	8,918	6,233	3,339	1,823	15,094	14,746	93	10	46	(14)	94	80	10	7
Ba Ria – Vung Tau	9,281	6,114	3,689	2,029	13,310	10,857	52	(103)	3	(127)	101	85	9	8

continued on next page

Table A4.5 continued

Province	Avg. Owners' Equity		Avg. Fixed Assets		Avg. Net Turnover		Avg. Pre-tax Profit		Avg. After Tax Profit		Payable per Employee		Contribution to Trade Union, Social Insurance, Health Insurance, Unemployment Insurance per Employee	
	Per SME	Per WSME	Per SME	Per WSME	Per SME	Per WSME	Per SME	Per WSME	Per SME	Per WSME	SMEs	WSMEs	SMEs	WSMEs
Ho Chi Minh	9,319	6,220	1,383	985	12,063	11,101	6	(25)	(37)	(53)	111	97	14	11
Mekong River Delta	**7,772**	**5,920**	**3,414**	**2,749**	**14,946**	**15,917**	**36**	**(53)**	**8**	**(73)**	**72**	**66**	**6**	**5**
Long An	13,602	9,488	7,960	5,908	19,562	20,720	189	11	135	(21)	94	88	12	12
Tien Giang	5,518	4,441	2,897	2,326	13,506	14,058	54	170	24	140	69	60	5	3
Ben Tre	4,582	3,385	2,852	2,052	15,992	14,200	45	(38)	29	(44)	74	74	4	3
Tra Vinh	10,968	3,659	2,030	1,771	13,881	16,204	79	52	60	40	58	51	5	4
Vinh Long	5,077	2,932	1,493	1,141	10,709	11,661	(48)	43	(77)	19	64	62	4	4
Dong Thap	5,400	4,173	1,716	1,476	14,445	16,658	216	210	181	173	76	53	7	3
An Giang	5,898	5,028	2,699	1,142	15,539	15,964	210	249	187	231	66	64	4	3
Kien Giang	8,311	8,133	3,741	3,188	10,576	11,106	(170)	(81)	(178)	(91)	69	64	2	2
Can Tho	6,657	5,059	2,021	2,436	12,631	17,071	15	39	(10)	25	65	59	5	5
Hau Giang	8,451	6,690	3,660	2,683	14,454	12,293	198	287	177	273	58	58	5	5
Soc Trang	6,658	5,486	2,696	3,105	16,576	13,493	(26)	128	(46)	102	59	55	8	3
Bac Lieu	10,022	9,708	2,577	2,982	15,809	24,330	(692)	(3,062)	(720)	(3,080)	62	60	3	3
Ca Mau	5,068	3,972	1,905	1,692	20,848	17,927	105	24	78	10	55	52	3	2

SMEs = small and medium-sized enterprises, WSMEs = women-owned small and medium-sized enterprises.
Source: General Statistics Office. 2021. Economic Census.

Table A4.6: Key Indicators of Women–Owned Small and Medium-Sized Enterprises Operating as of 31 December 2020 by Economic Sector
(D million)

Economic sector	Avg. Owners' Equity		Avg. Fixed Assets		Avg. Net Turnover		Avg. Pre-tax Profit		Avg. After Tax Profit		Payable per Employee		Contribution to Trade Union, Social Insurance, Health Insurance, Unemployment Insurance per Employee	
	Per SME	Per WSME	Per SME	Per WSME	Per SME	Per WSME	Per SME	Per WSME	Per SME	Per WSME	SMEs	WSMEs	SMEs	WSMEs
Whole country	**9,397**	**6,373**	**2,908**	**1,805**	**13,374**	**12,986**	**(13)**	**(45)**	**(48)**	**(66)**	**91**	**81**	**16**	**8**
Agriculture, forestry, and fishing	26,207	13,855	14,596	5,988	11,961	11,500	6	(108)	(25)	(132)	78	75	8	3
Mining and quarrying	19,871	13,101	9,369	8,270	18,165	16,816	290	82	129	49	86	84	9	7
Manufacturing	9,103	6,159	4,939	3,098	15,862	13,697	(73)	(146)	(113)	(167)	92	83	12	9
Electricity, gas, stream, and air conditioning supply	41,591	16,146	57,648	20,657	14,096	7,502	1,223	455	1,154	431	98	64	9	4
Water supply, sewerage, waste management, and remediation activities	18,978	20,114	13,320	5,081	10,494	4,784	305	15	246	2	92	70	12	7
Construction	10,023	9,440	1,947	1,692	11,118	10,440	8	27	(13)	11	83	75	5	4
Wholesale and retail trade; repair of motor vehicles and motorcycles	5,309	4,527	943	770	18,096	18,374	(49)	11	(71)	(7)	85	80	8	8
Transportation and storage	7,308	4,390	4,716	2,507	12,347	11,097	(13)	(122)	(50)	(142)	95	87	10	7

continued on next page

Table A4.6 continued

Economic sector	Avg. Owners' Equity		Avg. Fixed Assets		Avg. Net Turnover		Avg. Pre-tax Profit		Avg. After Tax Profit		Payable per Employee		Contribution to Trade Union, Social Insurance, Health Insurance, Unemployment Insurance per Employee	
	Per SME	Per WSME	Per SME	Per WSME	Per SME	Per WSME	Per SME	Per WSME	Per SME	Per WSME	SMEs	WSMEs	SMEs	WSMEs
Accommodation and food service activities	8,028	5,224	4,763	3,363	4,214	3,466	(607)	(420)	(615)	(424)	64	59	8	6
Information and communication	6,375	4,325	752	497	6,763	5,802	254	107	218	84	162	130	20	14
Financial, banking, and insurance activities	55,130	14,361	1,402	522	8,893	3,797	1,029	108	704	56	173	95	16	8
Real estate activities	82,247	49,428	12,762	11,530	12,940	9,328	1,014	411	710	257	120	107	14	11
Professional, scientific, and technical activities	6,478	5,629	697	387	4,260	3,416	93	73	65	55	116	97	126	9
Administrative and support service activities	6,485	4,118	1,448	653	4,733	4,176	(83)	(101)	(102)	(109)	84	79	7	7
Education and training	4,989	3,699	1,911	1,489	2,362	2,045	(312)	(224)	(321)	(232)	80	74	10	9
Human health and social work activities	7,935	6,181	3,397	2,715	6,010	4,242	(333)	(443)	(353)	(453)	91	86	10	10
Arts, entertainment, and recreation	13,226	7,277	2,935	2,656	4,981	2,756	(524)	(1,034)	(554)	(1,041)	85	71	11	8
Other service activities	3,577	2,693	830	780	2,855	2,129	(82)	(225)	(104)	(238)	68	65	8	8

( ) = negative, Avg. = average, SMEs = small and medium-sized enterprises, WSMEs = women-owned small and medium-sized enterprises.
Source: General Statistics Office. 2021. Economic Census.

Table A4.7: Women-Owned Small and Medium-Sized Enterprises Operating at a Profit, Loss, and Balance by Province

Province	SMEs (Number)	SMEs Operating at a (%)			WSMEs (Number)	WSMEs Operating at a (%)		
		Profit	Loss	Balance		Profit	Loss	Balance
Whole country	**523,124**	**48**	**49**	**3**	**105,876**	**46**	**52**	**2**
Northern Midlands and Mountain areas	**22,661**	**56**	**41**	**3**	**3,884**	**53**	**44**	**3**
Ha Giang	725	78	17	5	95	79	16	5
Cao Bang	793	79	17	3	160	78	20	3
Bac Kan	446	56	36	9	65	48	48	5
Tuyen Quang	1,020	71	26	3	181	71	27	2
Lao Cai	1,729	54	44	2	363	50	48	2
Dien Bien	747	77	19	5	182	79	19	3
Lai Chau	662	74	19	8	101	63	30	7
Son La	1,406	66	33	1	215	64	36	0
Yen Bai	1,132	62	36	2	209	54	44	1
Hoa Binh	1,440	51	43	6	234	50	44	6
Thai Nguyen	3,270	49	49	2	540	46	51	2
Lang Son	1,402	47	50	3	340	42	55	3
Bac Giang	4,199	42	55	3	635	40	58	2
Phu Tho	3,690	55	41	4	564	52	44	5
Red River Delta	**168,335**	**48**	**50**	**2**	**31,057**	**46**	**53**	**1**
Ha Noi	110,795	47	52	1	21,060	44	55	1
Quang Ninh	5,873	49	49	2	1184	47	51	2
Vinh Phuc	4,944	41	54	4	752	39	56	4
Bac Ninh	8,565	55	44	1	1703	53	46	1
Hai Duong	6,295	41	57	2	994	38	60	2
Hai Phong	12,924	58	41	1	2,460	59	40	1
Hung Yen	4,947	38	59	3	755	33	63	4
Thai Binh	3,434	44	53	3	545	40	58	2

continued on next page

Table A4.7 continued

Province	SMEs (Number)	SMEs Operating at a (%)			WSMEs (Number)	WSMEs Operating at a (%)		
		Profit	Loss	Balance		Profit	Loss	Balance
Ha Nam	3,047	49	48	3	434	47	51	2
Nam Dinh	4,495	64	32	4	700	65	30	5
Ninh Binh	3,016	50	46	4	470	47	49	4
Northern Central area and Central Coastal area	**71,865**	**48**	**47**	**5**	**13,705**	**44**	**52**	**4**
Thanh Hoa	7,985	66	30	5	1234	65	32	4
Nghe An	8,238	48	45	7	940	49	45	6
Ha Tinh	3,219	54	40	6	438	58	38	4
Quang Binh	3,042	45	51	5	498	37	60	3
Quang Tri	1,992	58	33	9	474	54	36	10
Thua Thien Hue	3,325	61	35	5	616	56	39	5
Da Nang	16,337	33	62	5	4076	30	66	5
Quang Nam	5,345	43	50	7	906	35	58	6
Quang Ngai	3,783	58	39	3	708	55	42	3
Binh Dinh	5,047	65	32	2	1040	63	35	2
Phu Yen	2,043	55	41	4	449	53	44	4
Khanh Hoa	6,656	36	63	1	1468	32	67	1
Ninh Thuan	1,744	50	46	4	296	42	55	3
Binh Thuan	3,109	46	49	5	562	49	46	5
Central Highlands	**14,238**	**48**	**46**	**5**	**3,126**	**45**	**50**	**6**
Kon Tum	1,126	69	29	2	264	66	32	2
Gia Lai	2,920	47	47	6	583	44	47	9
Dak Lak	4,534	48	47	5	897	41	54	5
Dak Nong	1,464	52	42	7	368	47	46	8
Lam Dong	4,194	44	51	5	1014	42	54	4
South East	**204,079**	**44**	**54**	**2**	**45,337**	**43**	**56**	**2**

continued on next page

Table A4.7 continued

Province	SMEs (Number)	SMEs Operating at a (%)			WSMEs (Number)	WSMEs Operating at a (%)		
		Profit	Loss	Balance		Profit	Loss	Balance
Binh Phuoc	3,346	53	40	7	758	52	41	6
Tay Ninh	2,859	61	33	6	626	59	36	5
Binh Duong	22,122	45	53	2	4511	45	53	2
Dong Nai	15,738	56	43	2	2,940	58	40	2
Ba Ria – Vung Tau	7,096	54	45	2	1452	53	46	2
Ho Chi Minh	152,918	42	57	1	35,050	40	58	1
Mekong River Delta	**41,926**	**63**	**31**	**6**	**8,767**	**63**	**31**	**5**
Long An	6,606	56	41	3	1268	57	40	2
Tien Giang	3,724	66	28	7	924	66	27	7
Ben Tre	2,477	55	39	6	525	53	43	4
Tra Vinh	1,591	72	23	5	306	69	26	4
Vinh Long	1,945	68	28	4	414	70	25	5
Dong Thap	2,749	68	27	5	635	69	26	5
An Giang	3,339	78	18	4	735	78	18	4
Kien Giang	5,272	52	40	8	1181	50	42	8
Can Tho	6,463	58	35	8	1118	57	36	7
Hau Giang	1,435	69	26	5	332	73	25	2
Soc Trang	2,104	70	21	9	363	73	23	4
Bac Lieu	1,592	59	26	15	349	60	26	14
Ca Mau	2,629	81	14	6	617	79	16	5

SMEs = small and medium-sized enterprises, WSMEs = women-owned small and medium-sized enterprises.
Source: General Statistics Office. 2021. Economic Census.

Table A4.8: Women-Owned Small and Medium-Sized Enterprises Operating at a Profit, Loss and Balance by Economic Sector

Economic sector	SMEs (Number)	SMEs Operating at a (%)			WSMEs (Number)	WSMEs Operating at a (%)		
		Profit	Loss	Balance		Profit	Loss	Balance
Whole country	**523,124**	**48**	**49**	**3**	**105,876**	**46**	**52**	**2**
Agriculture, forestry, and fishing	4,121	45	45	10	673	48	44	8
Mining and quarrying	2,239	53	41	6	267	53	42	6
Manufacturing	81,602	48	49	3	14,466	46	51	2
Electricity, gas, stream, and air conditioning supply	3,250	40	40	19	537	33	42	25
Water supply, sewerage, waste management, and remediation activities	2,043	52	44	4	331	45	51	3
Construction	71,747	57	38	4	7,099	57	38	5
Wholesale and retail trade; repair of motor vehicles and motorcycles	204,271	49	49	2	49,055	49	49	2
Transportation and storage	31,986	46	53	1	6,752	45	54	2
Accommodation and food service activities	19,142	27	71	2	5,977	27	71	2
Information and communication	11,030	50	48	2	1,562	50	48	1
Financial, banking, and insurance activities	2,240	47	48	5	632	46	51	3
Real estate activities	11,655	47	50	3	2,296	45	52	3
Professional, scientific, and technical activities	43,578	51	47	2	7,157	46	52	2
Administrative and support service activities	20,312	38	60	2	4,842	36	61	2
Education and training	6,127	28	69	3	2,283	28	69	3
Human health and social work activities	2,109	35	62	3	540	31	66	3
Arts, entertainment, and recreation	2,247	30	67	2	530	29	68	3
Other service activities	3,425	35	63	2	877	27	71	1

SMEs = small and medium-sized enterprises, WSMEs = women-owned small and medium-sized enterprises.
Source: General Statistics Office. 2021. Economic Census.

Table A4.9: Women-Owned Small and Medium-Sized Enterprises Operating as of 31 December 2020 Having Website and Export and Import Activities by Province (%)

Province	Having Website		Having Export and Import Activities	
	SMEs	WSMEs	SMEs	WSMEs
Whole country	**24**	**22**	**9**	**9**
Northern Midlands and Mountain areas	**13**	**12**	**6**	**8**
Ha Giang	5	3	3	1
Cao Bang	13	15	3	6
Bac Kan	12	13	1	5
Tuyen Quang	7	5	3	2
Lao Cai	9	9	8	12
Dien Bien	58	47	1	2
Lai Chau	3	3	1	0
Son La	10	11	3	2
Yen Bai	16	14	5	4
Hoa Binh	12	15	3	3
Thai Nguyen	19	14	4	3
Lang Son	8	6	23	34
Bac Giang	10	7	10	11
Phu Tho	12	11	6	6
Red River Delta	**35**	**32**	**11**	**11**
Ha Noi	46	42	12	12
Quang Ninh	13	10	5	5
Vinh Phuc	11	10	7	6
Bac Ninh	10	7	16	15
Hai Duong	12	9	8	10
Hai Phong	13	11	10	12
Hung Yen	19	17	12	13
Thai Binh	17	14	6	6
Ha Nam	4	4	8	7
Nam Dinh	6	5	4	5
Ninh Binh	8	9	5	5
Northern Central area and Central Coastal area	**14**	**13**	**3**	**3**
Thanh Hoa	6	5	2	2
Nghe An	15	15	2	4
Ha Tinh	13	10	4	6
Quang Binh	11	12	1	2
Quang Tri	8	7	4	5

continued on next page

Table A4.9 *continued*

Province	Having Website		Having Export and Import Activities	
	SMEs	WSMEs	SMEs	WSMEs
Thua Thien Hue	14	14		2
Da Nang	15	12	5	4
Quang Nam	22	21	2	3
Quang Ngai	12	12	2	2
Binh Dinh	17	17	4	4
Phu Yen	9	8	3	3
Khanh Hoa	18	17	2	2
Ninh Thuan	8	10	3	2
Binh Thuan	22	26	3	3
Central Highlands	**14**	**13**	**3**	**3**
Kon Tum	9	9	2	5
Gia Lai	19	17	3	3
Dak Lak	12	11	1	1
Dak Nong	7	6	1	1
Lam Dong	17	16	5	4
South East	**23**	**21**	**11**	**10**
Binh Phuoc	14	9	5	4
Tay Ninh	11	8	7	5
Binh Duong	17	14	12	13
Dong Nai	10	8	7	6
Ba Ria – Vung Tau	18	16	4	4
Ho Chi Minh	26	24	11	11
Mekong River Delta	**11**	**10**	**4**	**4**
Long An	20	18	13	12
Tien Giang	7	6	3	3
Ben Tre	11	10	4	6
Tra Vinh	4	3	2	2
Vinh Long	3	2	2	2
Dong Thap	9	10	2	2
An Giang	6	8	2	2
Kien Giang	12	12	1	1
Can Tho	13	13	1	2
Hau Giang	4	3	2	2
Soc Trang	8	8	0	1
Bac Lieu	20	20	3	5
Ca Mau	5	5	1	1

SMEs = small and medium-sized enterprises, WSMEs = women-owned small and medium-sized enterprises.

Source: General Statistics Office. 2021. Economic Census.

Table A4.10: Women-Owned Small and Medium-Sized Enterprises Operating as of 31 December 2020 Having Website and Export and Import Activities by Economic Sector
(%)

Province	Having Website		Having Export and Import Activities	
	SMEs	WSMEs	SMEs	WSMEs
Whole country	**24**	**22**	**9**	**9**
Agriculture, forestry, and fishing	20	18	7	7
Mining and quarrying	15	13	5	3
Manufacturing	26	23	16	15
Electricity, gas, stream, and air conditioning supply	10	7	5	5
Water supply, sewerage, waste management, and remediation activities	23	17	5	5
Construction	21	19	2	2
Wholesale and retail trade; repair of motor vehicles and motorcycles	23	21	12	12
Transportation and storage	22	22	7	7
Accommodation and food service activities	21	20	1	1
Information and communication	43	35	14	10
Financial, banking, and insurance activities	27	19	3	1
Real estate activities	29	25	2	1
Professional, scientific, and technical activities	27	26	4	3
Administrative and support service activities	29	27	4	3
Education and training	34	32	2	2
Human health and social work activities	31	32	2	2
Arts, entertainment, and recreation	23	22	2	1
Other service activities	22	20	2	3

SMEs = small and medium-sized enterprises, WSMEs = women-owned small and medium-sized enterprises.
Source: General Statistics Office. 2021. Economic Census.

Table A4.11: Women-Owned Small- and Medium-Sized Enterprises Participating in Some Activities and Receiving State Support by Province

Province	WSMEs Answered (Number)	Participating in Supply Chain, Industry Cluster, and Value Chains (%)		Having National Brand (%)	Having International Brand (%)	Having Products Certified for (%)		Receiving State Support in Branding Development (%)
		All	Of Which, Receiving State Support			National Certification	International Certification	
Whole country	**110,667**	**4**	**46**	**3**	**1**	**9**	**1**	**5**
Northern Midlands and Mountain areas	**4,086**	**7**	**53**	**4**	**1**	**13**	**1**	**7**
Ha Giang	98	7	29	1	1	8	1	4
Cao Bang	169	6	30	2	–	8	–	8
Bac Kan	68	16	73	13	1	34	1	13
Tuyen Quang	184	15	50	6	2	13	1	11
Lao Cai	409	8	41	8	1	15	2	9
Dien Bien	187	4	29	2	–	6	1	5
Lai Chau	111	10	91	3	–	12	–	12
Son La	216	8	89	6	–	16	0	9
Yen Bai	217	7	67	2	0	12	0	5
Hoa Binh	244	7	56	9	0	18	0	9
Thai Nguyen	562	4	70	3	1	12	1	5
Lang Son	356	8	31	4	1	15	1	4
Bac Giang	677	5	58	4	1	10	1	4
Phu Tho	588	7	45	3	1	12	1	6
Red River Delta	**32,459**	**4**	**42**	**3**	**1**	**9**	**1**	**5**
Ha Noi	21,936	4	42	3	1	10	2	5
Quang Ninh	1,230	4	33	5	1	11	0	6
Vinh Phuc	808	6	60	3	1	10	1	5

continued on next page

Table A4.11 continued

Province	WSMEs Answered (Number)	Participating in Supply Chain, Industry Cluster, and Value Chains (%)		Having National Brand (%)	Having International Brand (%)	Having Products Certified for (%)		Receiving State Support in Branding Development (%)
		All	Of Which, Receiving State Support			National Certification	International Certification	
Bac Ninh	1,802	4	38	1	0	6	1	3
Hai Duong	1,040	4	33	3	1	9	1	4
Hai Phong	2,599	4	28	2	0	8	1	3
Hung Yen	780	5	39	3	1	10	1	5
Thai Binh	602	12	52	8	1	18	1	10
Ha Nam	445	4	26	5	1	11	2	6
Nam Dinh	736	6	66	3	0	11	0	5
Ninh Binh	481	4	42	4	0	10	0	5
Northern Central area and Central Coastal area	**14,630**	**6**	**48**	**4**	**1**	**10**	**1**	**7**
Thanh Hoa	1,523	11	55	5	2	12	2	8
Nghe An	982	17	64	3	1	15	1	14
Ha Tinh	474	5	60	5	1	14	1	6
Quang Binh	528	11	74	8	3	16	3	9
Quang Tri	524	6	45	1	0	7	0	19
Thua Thien Hue	662	6	38	5	2	13	2	9
Da Nang	4,197	3	21	3	1	8	1	3
Quang Nam	974	8	44	3	1	13	1	6
Quang Ngai	737	4	30	6	1	11	0	6
Binh Dinh	1,080	3	35	2	0	8	0	4

continued on next page

Table A4.11 continued

| Province | WSMEs Answered (Number) | Participating in Supply Chain, Industry Cluster, and Value Chains (%) | | Having National Brand (%) | Having International Brand (%) | Having Products Certified for (%) | | Receiving State Support in Branding Development (%) |
		All	Of Which, Receiving State Support			National Certification	International Certification	
Phu Yen	463	5	24	4	0	13	1	5
Khanh Hoa	1,597	3	40	3	0	8	0	4
Ninh Thuan	304	5	50	3	1	11	-	8
Binh Thuan	585	9	58	3	0	13	1	9
Central Highlands	**3,264**	**8**	**46**	**6**	**1**	**14**	**1**	**8**
Kon Tum	268	16	70	14	1	29	1	26
Gia Lai	606	7	48	5	1	15	1	9
Dak Lak	960	7	31	9	2	15	2	4
Dak Nong	378	6	58	1	-	6	0	8
Lam Dong	1,052	7	40	4	1	12	1	7
South East	**47,238**	**3**	**40**	**2**	**1**	**6**	**1**	**4**
Binh Phuoc	790	5	41	3	1	9	1	6
Tay Ninh	644	2	33	2	0	6	-	3
Binh Duong	4,569	3	39	1	0	5	1	4
Dong Nai	3,054	6	66	2	0	6	0	7
Ba Ria – Vung Tau	1,551	3	24	2	0	5	1	2
Ho Chi Minh	36,630	3	36	2	1	6	1	3
Mekong River Delta	**8,990**	**7**	**60**	**3**	**0**	**12**	**1**	**8**

continued on next page

Table A4.11 *continued*

Province	WSMEs Answered (Number)	Participating in Supply Chain, Industry Cluster, and Value Chains (%)		Having National Brand (%)	Having International Brand (%)	Having Products Certified for (%)		Receiving State Support in Branding Development (%)
		All	Of Which, Receiving State Support			National Certification	International Certification	
Long An	1,278	4	48	2	0	10	0	4
Tien Giang	943	8	63	3	0	11	0	6
Ben Tre	534	3	47	3	0	10	1	4
Tra Vinh	310	6	65	3	1	9	1	7
Vinh Long	425	4	58	2	0	11	0	7
Dong Thap	657	8	63	4	0	14	0	12
An Giang	755	3	36	2	0	9	1	3
Kien Giang	1,212	12	50	7	0	17	0	8
Can Tho	1,142	10	61	3	1	15	1	10
Hau Giang	347	19	88	5	0	16	1	30
Soc Trang	372	5	50	2	–	9	–	10
Bac Lieu	368	10	87	3	–	13	–	9
Ca Mau	647	3	42	4	0	7	0	4

WSMEs = women–owned small and medium–sized enterprises.
Source: General Statistics Office. 2021. Economic Census.

Table A4.12: Women-Owned Small and Medium-Sized Enterprises Participating in Some Activities and Receiving State Support by Province (continued)

Province	WSMEs Answered (Number)	Having Activities to Innovate, Improve Products, Services, Processes, and Business Models (%)	Receiving State Support When Implementing Innovation Activities (%)	Participating in State-Supported Training Programs to Improve Quality of Human Resources (%)		Transformed from Household Business (%)		Implemented Digital Transformation (%)	Having Digital Transformation Plan in Future (%)
				All	Of Which, Receiving State Support	All	Of Which, Receiving State Support		
Whole country	**110,667**	**12**	**19**	**2**	**51**	**3**	**62**	**28**	**13**
Northern Midlands and Mountain areas	**4,086**	**12**	**24**	**4**	**51**	**5**	**57**	**32**	**14**
Ha Giang	98	6	83	4	25	2	50	35	13
Cao Bang	169	9	38	3	60	4	29	34	16
Bac Kan	68	12	38	4	67	7	60	29	18
Tuyen Quang	184	14	32	7	25	5	78	46	22
Lao Cai	409	8	15	3	55	2	60	25	9
Dien Bien	187	8	33	2	67	10	37	60	5
Lai Chau	111	20	45	8	78	5	67	30	21
Son La	216	12	15	7	50	5	70	40	20
Yen Bai	217	17	25	3	57	8	78	35	12
Hoa Binh	244	11	33	3	43	7	61	31	17
Thai Nguyen	562	13	23	2	38	4	65	36	15
Lang Son	356	11	20	6	45	6	57	33	16
Bac Giang	677	13	17	5	59	5	66	22	11
Phu Tho	588	11	20	3	55	6	33	28	12

continued on next page

Table A4.12 continued

Province	WSMEs Answered (Number)	Having Activities to Innovate, Improve Products, Services, Processes, and Business Models (%)	Receiving State Support When Implementing Innovation Activities (%)	Participating in State-Supported Training Programs to Improve Quality of Human Resources (%)		Transformed from Household Business (%)		Implemented Digital Transformation (%)	Having Digital Transformation Plan in Future (%)
				All	Of Which, Receiving State Support	All	Of Which, Receiving State Support		
Red River Delta	**32,459**	**14**	**16**	**2**	**45**	**2**	**55**	**44**	**17**
Ha Noi	21,936	14	14	3	42	1	47	53	19
Quang Ninh	1,230	11	38	3	54	4	77	23	11
Vinh Phuc	808	16	15	3	54	6	85	26	13
Bac Ninh	1,802	13	16	2	50	4	66	23	11
Hai Duong	1,040	10	18	2	44	4	62	21	12
Hai Phong	2,599	10	20	2	62	3	42	23	12
Hung Yen	780	18	20	2	28	6	47	27	18
Thai Binh	602	19	24	2	57	6	62	33	20
Ha Nam	445	18	14	3	43	5	54	22	12
Nam Dinh	736	13	20	2	50	8	44	30	21
Ninh Binh	481	13	17	3	62	6	52	28	15
Northern Central area and Central Coastal area	**14,630**	**11**	**24**	**3**	**60**	**5**	**71**	**24**	**13**
Thanh Hoa	1,523	16	25	4	67	8	79	23	11
Nghe An	982	14	42	4	43	5	62	30	19
Ha Tinh	474	11	43	6	67	6	73	24	15
Quang Binh	528	18	21	5	86	9	74	28	14

continued on next page

Table A4.12 continued

Province	WSMEs Answered (Number)	Having Activities to Innovate, Improve Products, Services, Processes, and Business Models (%)	Receiving State Support When Implementing Innovation Activities (%)	Participating in State-Supported Training Programs to Improve Quality of Human Resources (%)		Transformed from Household Business (%)		Implemented Digital Transformation (%)	Having Digital Transformation Plan in Future (%)
				All	Of Which, Receiving State Support	All	Of Which, Receiving State Support		
Quang Tri	524	8	29	2	75	5	54	28	11
Thua Thien Hue	662	14	24	4	59	11	59	29	13
Da Nang	4,197	9	14	1	50	1	59	22	11
Quang Nam	974	11	22	3	52	5	82	29	15
Quang Ngai	737	8	15	3	60	11	77	23	11
Binh Dinh	1,080	14	21	3	56	4	77	20	14
Phu Yen	463	13	21	3	31	11	61	24	16
Khanh Hoa	1,597	7	28	2	67	2	72	21	14
Ninh Thuan	304	12	31	4	50	4	50	24	12
Binh Thuan	585	12	29	4	76	8	77	31	15
Central Highlands	**3,264**	**12**	**28**	**4**	**57**	**7**	**61**	**27**	**13**
Kon Tum	268	25	26	4	67	14	43	38	19
Gia Lai	606	10	29	3	52	4	74	23	11
Dak Lak	960	8	18	3	45	7	66	33	15
Dak Nong	378	14	27	4	64	7	73	18	12
Lam Dong	1,052	14	34	4	63	7	55	23	12
South East	**47,238**	**11**	**16**	**1**	**43**	**1**	**50**	**19**	**10**
Binh Phuoc	790	10	20	1	67	6	63	22	12

continued on next page

Table A4.12 continued

Province	WSMEs Answered (Number)	Having Activities to Innovate, Improve Products, Services, Processes, and Business Models (%)	Receiving State Support When Implementing Innovation Activities (%)	Participating in State-Supported Training Programs to Improve Quality of Human Resources (%)		Transformed from Household Business (%)		Implemented Digital Transformation (%)	Having Digital Transformation Plan in Future (%)
				All	Of Which, Receiving State Support	All	Of Which, Receiving State Support		
Tay Ninh	644	5	22	2	33	4	60	12	7
Binh Duong	4,569	15	15	1	53	1	48	15	10
Dong Nai	3,054	14	35	2	59	1	60	19	10
Ba Ria – Vung Tau	1,551	5	15	1	47	3	70	15	5
Ho Chi Minh	36,630	10	14	1	40	1	43	20	11
Mekong River Delta	**8,990**	**12**	**35**	**2**	**73**	**6**	**73**	**21**	**11**
Long An	1,278	12	22	2	41	4	54	20	9
Tien Giang	943	7	25	2	71	6	78	17	9
Ben Tre	534	12	15	1	50	7	56	16	9
Tra Vinh	310	9	31	1	100	11	71	18	5
Vinh Long	425	10	39	3	82	6	50	17	7
Dong Thap	657	19	49	4	83	13	82	33	17
An Giang	755	7	31	3	64	4	59	12	8
Kien Giang	1,212	13	33	2	58	6	87	19	18
Can Tho	1,142	11	42	2	82	3	69	32	10
Hau Giang	347	22	64	7	83	7	92	33	15
Soc Trang	372	8	57	3	100	7	72	29	12
Bac Lieu	368	30	28	5	88	5	100	23	18
Ca Mau	647	2	29	2	100	3	61	11	9

WSMEs = women-owned small and medium-sized enterprises.
Source: General Statistics Office. 2021. Economic Census.

Table A4.13: Women-Owned Small and Medium-Sized Enterprises Participating in Some Activities and Receiving State Support by Economic Sector

Province	WSMEs Answered (Number)	Participating in Supply Chain, Industry Cluster, and Value Chains (%)		Having National Brand (%)	Having International Brand (%)	Having Products Certified for (%)		Receiving State Support in Branding Development (%)
		All	Of Which, Receiving State Support			National Certification	International Certification	
Whole country	**110,667**	**4**	**46**	**3**	**1**	**9**	**1**	**5**
Agriculture, forestry, and fishing	726	11	56	4	0	13	1	10
Mining and quarrying	289	7	26	1	–	10	–	5
Manufacturing	15,025	6	50	3	0	11	1	6
Electricity, gas, stream, and air conditioning supply	563	7	58	2	–	8	–	7
Water supply, sewerage, waste management, and remediation activities	341	3	40	1	0	7	0	3
Construction	7,441	5	45	1	0	4	0	5
Wholesale and retail trade; repair of motor vehicles and motorcycles	51,041	5	47	4	1	11	2	5
Transportation and storage	7,045	4	38	1	0	2	0	3
Accommodation and food service activities	6,372	4	46	1	0	10	0	4
Information and communication	1,639	4	33	2	0	4	0	5
Financial, banking, and insurance activities	670	7	52	6	3	10	3	8
Real estate activities	2,425	4	37	1	0	2	0	5
Professional, scientific, and technical activities	7,422	3	46	1	0	4	0	4
Administrative and support service activities	5,134	4	34	1	0	4	0	4
Education and training	2,466	3	40	2	1	8	1	5
Human health and social work activities	557	4	50	4	1	16	1	6
Arts, entertainment, and recreation	567	3	35	1	1	2	1	3
Other service activities	944	2	50	1	1	5	1	3

WSMEs = women-owned small and medium-sized enterprises.
Source: General Statistics Office. 2021. Economic Census.

Table A4.14: Women–Owned Small and Medium–Sized Enterprises Participating in Some Activities and Receiving State Support by Economic Sector (continued)

Province	WSMEs Answered (Number)	Having Activities to Innovate, Improve Products, Services, Processes, and Business Models (%)	Receiving State Support When Implementing Innovation Activities (%)	Participating in State-Supported Training Programs to Improve Quality of Human Resources (%)		Transformed from Household Business (%)		Implemented Digital Transformation (%)	Having Digital Transformation Plan in Future (%)
				All	Of Which, Receiving State Support	All	Of Which, Receiving State Support		
Whole country	**110,667**	**12**	**19**	**2**	**51**	**3**	**62**	**28**	**13**
Agriculture, forestry, and fishing	726	14	43	3	76	5	67	21	11
Mining and quarrying	289	11	33	3	50	3	40	26	11
Manufacturing	15,025	19	19	2	51	3	60	26	14
Electricity, gas, stream, and air conditioning supply	563	10	33	4	60	2	75	27	14
Water supply, sewerage, waste management, and remediation activities	341	10	33	2	29	4	57	21	11
Construction	7,441	10	21	2	49	1	75	27	12
Wholesale and retail trade; repair of motor vehicles and motorcycles	51,041	10	19	2	50	4	62	28	13
Transportation and storage	7,045	8	18	2	46	1	60	26	12
Accommodation and food service activities	6,372	9	20	2	62	3	63	23	10

continued on next page

Table A4.14 continued

Province	WSMEs Answered (Number)	Having Activities to Innovate, Improve Products, Services, Processes, and Business Models (%)	Receiving State Support When Implementing Innovation Activities (%)	Participating in State-Supported Training Programs to Improve Quality of Human Resources (%)		Transformed from Household Business (%)		Implemented Digital Transformation (%)	Having Digital Transformation Plan in Future (%)
				All	Of Which, Receiving State Support	All	Of Which, Receiving State Support		
Information and communication	1,639	17	18	2	52	1	44	40	20
Financial, banking, and insurance activities	670	15	21	3	52	1	60	31	14
Real estate activities	2,425	8	20	2	52	1	65	28	12
Professional, scientific, and technical activities	7,422	11	16	2	43	1	59	30	15
Administrative and support service activities	5,134	11	16	2	53	1	52	28	13
Education and training	2,466	16	19	5	56	1	65	29	14
Human health and social work activities	557	15	24	6	47	3	64	42	20
Arts, entertainment, and recreation	567	10	7	2	50	1	63	23	11
Other service activities	944	10	15	1	43	2	35	20	10

WSMEs = women-owned small and medium-sized enterprises.
Source: General Statistics Office. 2021. Economic Census.

Table A4.15: Women-Owned Small and Medium-Sized Enterprises Having Loan and Demand for Loan by Province

Province	WSMEs Answered (Number)	Having Loans for Production and Business Activities (%)	Having Access to Preferential Credit (%)	Having Demand for Loan from Credit Institutions to Serve Production and Business Activities in Coming Time (%)	Having Demand for Seeking Investment Capital Resources from Investors to Serve Production and Business Activities in Coming Time (%)
Whole country	**110,667**	**20**	**6**	**26**	**20**
Northern Midlands and Mountain areas	**4,086**	**31**	**12**	**40**	**31**
Ha Giang	98	30	14	35	28
Cao Bang	169	35	20	41	32
Bac Kan	68	37	21	38	32
Tuyen Quang	184	33	17	43	38
Lao Cai	409	20	8	29	18
Dien Bien	187	37	12	49	28
Lai Chau	111	37	15	61	50
Son La	216	32	13	44	33
Yen Bai	217	35	12	41	31
Hoa Binh	244	28	10	45	39
Thai Nguyen	562	38	14	43	36
Lang Son	356	33	10	43	31
Bac Giang	677	24	8	31	23
Phu Tho	588	33	15	42	31
Red River Delta	**32,459**	**22**	**6**	**29**	**24**
Ha Noi	21,936	20	5	27	24
Quang Ninh	1,230	25	8	28	22
Vinh Phuc	808	32	13	45	38
Bac Ninh	1,802	24	6	30	23

continued on next page

Table A4.15 continued

Province	WSMEs Answered (Number)	Having Loans for Production and Business Activities (%)	Having Access to Preferential Credit (%)	Having Demand for Loan from Credit Institutions to Serve Production and Business Activities in Coming Time (%)	Having Demand for Seeking Investment Capital Resources from Investors to Serve Production and Business Activities in Coming Time (%)
Hai Duong	1,040	22	7	31	25
Hai Phong	2,599	22	6	27	20
Hung Yen	780	31	10	39	31
Thai Binh	602	34	11	46	35
Ha Nam	445	29	11	39	34
Nam Dinh	736	22	10	32	28
Ninh Binh	481	38	10	42	31
Northern Central area and Central Coastal area	**14,630**	**26**	**9**	**33**	**23**
Thanh Hoa	1,523	26	13	36	31
Nghe An	982	32	14	37	29
Ha Tinh	474	29	10	39	27
Quang Binh	528	31	9	40	31
Quang Tri	524	39	14	45	31
Thua Thien Hue	662	33	11	39	29
Da Nang	4,197	21	5	23	14
Quang Nam	974	32	15	40	28
Quang Ngai	737	29	9	34	24
Binh Dinh	1,080	27	8	33	19
Phu Yen	463	25	10	34	23
Khanh Hoa	1,597	18	7	34	25
Ninh Thuan	304	39	12	38	28
Binh Thuan	585	28	11	32	21

continued on next page

Table A4.15 *continued*

Province	WSMEs Answered (Number)	Having Loans for Production and Business Activities (%)	Having Access to Preferential Credit (%)	Having Demand for Loan from Credit Institutions to Serve Production and Business Activities in Coming Time (%)	Having Demand for Seeking Investment Capital Resources from Investors to Serve Production and Business Activities in Coming Time (%)
Central Highlands	**3,264**	**31**	**12**	**37**	**28**
Kon Tum	268	26	13	38	38
Gia Lai	606	33	11	36	25
Dak Lak	960	34	11	39	27
Dak Nong	378	40	16	48	35
Lam Dong	1,052	25	10	32	24
South East	47,238	14	3	20	14
Binh Phuoc	790	33	10	45	24
Tay Ninh	644	22	6	24	13
Binh Duong	4,569	13	4	18	13
Dong Nai	3,054	21	7	28	17
Ba Ria – Vung Tau	1,551	13	5	17	12
Ho Chi Minh	36,630	13	3	19	14
Mekong River Delta	**8,990**	**21**	**9**	**32**	**22**
Long An	1,278	18	6	31	16
Tien Giang	943	21	8	31	24
Ben Tre	534	20	7	22	9
Tra Vinh	310	19	10	31	14
Vinh Long	425	24	7	28	16
Dong Thap	657	27	12	35	25
An Giang	755	16	6	26	18

continued on next page

Table A4.15 *continued*

Province	WSMEs Answered (Number)	Having Loans for Production and Business Activities (%)	Having Access to Preferential Credit (%)	Having Demand for Loan from Credit Institutions to Serve Production and Business Activities in Coming Time (%)	Having Demand for Seeking Investment Capital Resources from Investors to Serve Production and Business Activities in Coming Time (%)
Kien Giang	1,212	25	8	46	38
Can Tho	1,142	16	8	28	22
Hau Giang	347	12	6	33	29
Soc Trang	372	16	13	24	20
Bac Lieu	368	41	29	53	21
Ca Mau	647	27	6	31	14

WSMEs = women-owned small and medium-sized enterprises.
Source: General Statistics Office. 2021. Economic Census.

Table A4.16: Women–Owned Small and Medium–Sized Enterprises Having Loan and Demand for Loan by Economic Sector

Province	WSMEs answered (Number)	Having Loans for Production and Business activities (%)	Having Access to Preferential Credit (%)	Having Demand for Loan from Credit Institutions to Serve Production and Business Activities in Coming Time (%)	Having Demand for Seeking Investment Capital Resources from Investors to Serve Production and Business Activities in Coming Time (%)
Whole country	**110,667**	**20**	**6**	**26**	**20**
Agriculture, forestry, and fishing	726	32	11	43	30
Mining and quarrying	289	34	12	38	25
Manufacturing	15,025	23	7	30	23
Electricity, gas, stream, and air conditioning supply	563	41	15	38	28
Water supply, sewerage, waste management, and remediation activities	341	18	8	24	17
Construction	7,441	24	8	36	27
Wholesale and retail trade; repair of motor vehicles and motorcycles	51,041	22	7	28	20
Transportation and storage	7,045	23	7	27	19
Accommodation and food service activities	6,372	12	4	19	15
Information and communication	1,639	9	2	15	17
Financial, banking, and insurance activities	670	12	4	19	18
Real estate activities	2,425	17	5	22	19
Professional, scientific, and technical activities	7,422	9	2	16	15
Administrative and support service activities	5,134	11	3	18	17
Education and training	2,466	9	3	15	16
Human health and social work activities	557	13	5	20	18
Arts, entertainment, and recreation	567	10	2	19	18
Other service activities	944	9	2	16	14

WSMEs = women–owned small and medium–sized enterprises.
Source: General Statistics Office. 2021. Economic Census.

APPENDIX 5
Government Institutions Involved in SME Policy and Implementation and Key Legal and Policy Documents Related to SMEs and WSMEs

The table below details all relevant institutions, agencies, and ministries of the Government of Viet Nam involved in policymaking and implementation for small and medium-sized enterprises (SME) and women-owned SME support.[2]

Ministry/Agency	Responsibility Regarding (W)SME Support
Ministry of Planning and Investment (MPI)	MPI has the main responsibility for national SME policy, formulating and executing plans for SME assistance, training officials and employees in SME policy, and reporting to the government and Prime Minister on the implementation of SME policy. It is also responsible for the delivery of the SME Development Fund, SME Assistance Portal and database, and online training systems.
Agency for Enterprise Development (AED)	Under the MPI, AED is designated as the central government agency coordinating SME policy.
Assistance Centers for SMEs (former Technical Assistance Centers, TACs)	Managed by the AED, the three TACs of Ha Noi (North), Ho Chi Minh City (South), and Da Nang (Center) have the mission in their respective regions to organize and implement SME support policies and programs, including management training and business incubators.
Ministry of Finance (MOF)	MOF provides funding for SME assistance and guidelines for the use of regular funding from the state budget for provision of assistance to SMEs. It also provides (i) instructions on tax administrative procedures and the accounting regime for SMEs; (ii) has responsibility for establishing preferential tax policies and incentives for SMEs and innovative start-ups; (iii) provides support for conversion from household businesses to formal enterprises; (iv) develops SME Guarantee Fund regulations; and (v) supervises the financial performance of the Viet Nam Development Bank (VDB).
Ministry of Industry and Trade (MOIT)	MOIT implements the Program on the Development of Supporting Industries 2016–2025; instructs SMEs on how to join business clusters and value chains; promotes seminars to help SMEs participate in the distribution system; coordinates with existing medium-sized and large retailers in the domestic market. This Ministry also operates the Industrial Promotion Centers and the Trade Promotion Centers in each of the 63 provinces and is responsible for national export promotion efforts through the Viet Nam Trade Promotion Agency (VIETRADE).

continued on next page

---

2   https://www.oecd-ilibrary.org/sites/30c79519-en/1/3/4/index.html?itemId=/content/publication/30c79519-en&_csp_=85ee2ec32db3dbe99d71d2086df74f1f&itemIGO=oecd&itemContentType=book.

Table *continued*

Ministry/Agency	Responsibility Regarding (W)SME Support
Ministry of Science and Technology (MOST)	MOST is responsible for funding the National Innovative Startup Ecosystem to 2025 Scheme, among other duties. It provides instructions on the establishment of incubators; helps SMEs strengthening their technological capacity; supports links between SMEs and research institutes and universities; provides science and technology information for SMEs; and provides grants and preferential loans for R&D, innovation, and technology transfer.
National Agency for Technology Entrepreneurship and Commercialisation Development (NATEC)	Under MOST, this agency advises and assists the minister on developing the technology market and supporting the establishment and development of science and technology enterprises. It shares responsibilities for the implementation of the National Innovative Startup Ecosystem, creating a national start-up portal to link policymaking agencies, ministries, localities, start-up incubators, investors, and start-up businesses within this ecosystem.
Ministry of Information and Communications (MIC)	MIC introduces SMEs to e-commerce, and digital transformation and facilitates their access to online platforms.
Ministry of Education and Training (MOET)	MOET implements the "Supporting Student Entrepreneurship 2017–2020 with a Vision toward 2025" plan to equip students in educational and training establishments with knowledge and skills on entrepreneurship.
Ministry of Labour, Invalids and Social Affairs (MOLISA)	MOLISA is responsible for the Technical and Vocational Education and Training (TVET) system. It implements a strategic TVET plan to integrate entrepreneurship education at vocational colleges and schools, including teacher training programs, entrepreneurship training for students, and development of training materials and knowledge resources. MOLISA also has prime responsibility for guiding the support of vocational training for laborer's working in SMEs.
Ministry of Justice (MOJ)	MOJ provides legal information and advice for SMEs, as per Decree No. 55/2019/ND-CP dated 24 June 2019.
State Bank of Vietnam (SBV)	SBV organizes the implementation of government policies to increase the volume of SME lending. As part of this it supervises the collaboration of credit institutions and the Credit Guarantee Fund in implementing the credit guarantee mechanism.
Vietnam Development Bank (VDB)	Established in 2006, VDB implements the government's investment and export credit policies.
Vietnam Women's Union (VWU)	VWU is a sociopolitical organization representing the legal and legitimate rights and interests of Vietnamese women of all strata. The VWU strives for women's development and gender equality. The VWU has been assigned as the focal agency to implement the project "Supporting women start-up in the period of 2017–2025" (Project 939 approved by the Prime Minister on 30 June 2017).
Vietnam Youth Federation Supporting Centre for Youth Start-ups (SYS)	SYS implements the National Youth Startup Programme 2016–2021 to foster start-up activities among young people in collaboration with the Vietnam Chamber of Commerce and Industry (VCCI).
Central Institute of Economic Management (CIEM)	CIEM is the think-tank for the MPI. It undertakes analysis on enterprise and SME development and drafts laws, including the SME Support Law and the Enterprise Law.

continued on next page

Table *continued*

Ministry/Agency	Responsibility Regarding (W)SME Support
People's Provincial Councils	Councils introduce policies and distribute resources to help SMEs in provinces and supervise compliance with the SME Support Law at the provincial level.
People's Provincial Committees	Committees formulate, implement, and evaluate plans for assistance to SMEs in the provinces. Priority is given, in line with national guidelines, to supporting innovative start-ups, promoting household businesses to transform into legally registered enterprises, and encouraging SMEs to join clusters and value chains.

The following section provides brief summaries of each of the 11 policy and legal documents under review. It presents information on objectives, implementing agencies, targeted beneficiaries, and results indicators, if available. The section is structured to first present documents with explicit reference to women-owned SMEs and those that refer only to SMEs more broadly.

Specific to Women in Business

SME Law

Law 04/2017/QH14 on Support for Small- and Medium-sized (SME Law) was passed in 2017, coming into effect on 1 January 2018. The law represents the most significant piece of Vietnamese legislation targeted specifically at support for SMEs and includes various measures, provisions, and responsibilities across several ministries, agencies, and organizations of government. The SME Law is notable for providing the first clear definition of women-owned enterprises. Under Article 3, a women-owned SME is defined as an SME having one or more women owning at least 51% of its charter capital, and at least one woman serving as the executive director of the enterprise.

Objectives. To support the development of SMEs under categories of (i) access to credit and loans; (ii) access to credit guarantees; (iii) tax and accounting support; (iv) production space; (v) technology, start-up incubation, technical facilities, and co-working space; (vi) market expansion; (vii) access to information, consultancy, and legal advice; (viii) human resource development; (ix) transforming household businesses to enterprises; (x) assistance to innovative start-up SMEs and investment in innovative start-up SMEs; and (xi) assistance for SMEs participating in value chains and business clusters.

Implementing agencies. Ministry of Planning and Investment, Ministry of Finance, State Bank of Viet Nam, Ministry of Industry and Trade, Ministry of Justice, Ministry of Labor, War Invalids and Social Affairs

Associated decrees and circulars

Box A5: Associated Decrees and Circulars to SME Support Law

The government issued eight decrees for guiding the implementation of Law 04/2017/QH14 On Support for Small- and Medium-sized Enterprises, which cover nine groups of assistance measures for SMEs, SMEs in conversion from a household business, and SMEs participating in value chain and business clusters:

Credit Guarantee Fund

- Decree No. 34/2018/ND-CP on the establishment, organization, and operation of the Credit Guarantee Fund for SMEs, aimed at guiding the implementation of supporting SMEs to access credit through the Credit Guarantee Fund

Access to Credit

- Decree No. 80/2021/ND-CP dated 26 August 2021 providing guidance for the SME Law, replacing Decree No. 39/2018/ND-CP

Access to financing via SME Development Fund

- Decree No. 39/2019/ND-CP on organization and operation of the SMEDF to provide finance for innovative start-up SMEs and SMEs participating in value chains and business clusters

Tax and accounting support

- Decree No. 22/2020/ND-CP dated 24 February 2020 amending and supplementing a number of articles of Decree No. 139/2016/ND-CP dated 4 October 2016 on license fees

- Decree No. 41/2020/ND-CP dated 8 April 2020 to ease the tax burden for those facing difficulties due to the impact of COVID-19

Technology, start-up incubation, technical facilities, and co-working space

- Decree No. 37/2020/ND-CP on supplementing the list and industries with SME incubation, technical support facilities and co-working space for innovative start-up SMEs which would receive investment incentives, enjoy preferential policies on investment, specific incentives for CIT, and exemptions and reductions on land and water surface rent.

Investment in innovative start-up SMEs

- Decree No. 38/2018/ND-CP detailing investment for innovative start-up SMEs to guide and encourage start-up through start-up funds

    Decree No. 80/2021/NÐ-CP dated 26/8/2021 providing guidance for Supporting innovative start-up SMEs, support for SMEs participating in value chains and business clusters, support for SMEs in conversion from household businesses, support for SMEs (access to information, technology, consultancy, human resource development), grant compensation interest for innovative start-up SME, and SME participating in value chains

- Decree No. 39/2018/ND-CP specifically to guide its implementation of the SME Law

- Decree No. 80/2021/ND-CP dated 26/8/2021 providing guidance for the SME Law, replacing Decree No. 39/2018/ND-CP Decree No. 80/2021/ND-CP of the Government detailed regulations and instructions for implementing a number of articles of the SME.

continued on next page

Box A5 *continued*

Access to legal advices

- Decree No. 55/2019/ND-CP on legal support for SMEs, issued by the government on 24 June 2019 stipulates the principles of implementing legal support activities

Assistance for SMEs in conversion from household businesses

- Decree No. 108/2018/ND-CP dated 23 August 2018 to amend and supplement a number of articles of Decree No. 78/2015/ND-CP dated 14 September 2015 (replaced by Decree No. 01/2021/ND-CP dated 04 January 2021), regarding regulation on registration of business establishment on the basis of conversion from household business.

- Decree No. 80/2021/ND-CP dated 26/8/2021 providing guidance for the SME Law, replacing Decree No. 39/2018/ND-CP Decree No. 80/2021/ND-CP of the Government detailed regulations and instructions for implementing a number of articles of the SME.

Assistance for innovative start-up SMEs and SMEs participating in value chains and business clusters

- Decree No. 80/2021/ND-CP dated 26/8/2021 providing guidance for the SME Law, replacing Decree No. 39/2018/ND-CP

The Government of Viet Nam, the Prime Minister, and many ministries have issued decrees and circulars aimed at guiding and boosting the implementation of support measures identified in Article 8 to Article 20 of the SME Law.

Source: Asian Development Bank.

Target beneficiaries. Micro, small, and medium-sized enterprises including women-owned micro-small enterprises, and small and medium-sized enterprises (SMEs) including women-owned microenterprises.

Results indicators/Targets. None.

The National Gender Equality Strategy

Approval of the newly drafted National Gender Equality Strategy 2021–2030 of the Government of Viet Nam was enacted through Resolution No. 28/NQ-CP on 3 March 2021. The stated purpose of the new strategy is to "Continue to narrow gender gaps, create conditions, opportunities for women and men to participate, equally enjoy achievement in all spheres of society and life, and contribute to the sustainable development of the country." The updated version of the strategy was drafted with assistance from UN Women and the Australian Embassy in Viet Nam to replace the previous 2011–2020 national strategy document.

Objectives. (i) to intensify women's participation in managerial and leading positions to gradually narrow gender gaps in the political field; (ii) to narrow gender gaps in the economic, labor, and employment domains; (iii) to increase access of rural poor women and ethnic minority women to economic resources and labor market; (iv) to raise the quality of women human resources, and gradually ensure equal participation in the education and training between men and women; (v) to ensure gender equality in access to and benefit from healthcare services; (vi) to ensure gender equality in the cultural and information domain;

(vii) to ensure gender equality in family life, gradually eliminating gender-based violence; and (viii) to enhance capacity of gender equality state management.

Implementing agencies. Ministry of Labor, Invalids and Social Affairs

Associated decrees and circulars. Resolution No. 28/NQ-CP

Target beneficiaries. Women, WSMEs

Results indicators/Targets. The National Gender Equality Strategy 2021–2030 includes 20 specific targets relating to women in all aspects of socioeconomic and political life.

Law on Gender Equality

The *Law on Gender Equality* was enacted by the National Assembly in November 2006 coming into effect from 1 July 2007. This law is the first separate legal document regulating gender equality in the Vietnamese legal system and works to clarify legal definitions and expectations for gender equality. The law requests for the application of gender equality in all fields of social and family life including politics, economy, labor, education, science and technology, culture, information, physical training, and sports.

Objectives. (i) Institutionalizing the views of Viet Nam on women's liberation and creating opportunities and conditions for both men and women for contributing to the common development of the country; (ii) concretizing the constitutional principle of equality between men and women, without discriminating between men and women; (iii) systematizing the provisions of the current Law on Gender Equality; (iv) determining gender equality principles, responsibilities of agencies, organizations, families, and individuals for law formulation and implementation of gender equality; and (v) internalizing international treaties on gender equality that Viet Nam is a member, especially the Convention on the Elimination of all Forms of Discrimination Against Women.

Implementing agencies. Ministry of Labor, War Invalids and Social Affairs is the primary implementing agency, but the law includes stipulations that apply to all levels of Vietnamese governance.

Associated decrees and circulars. Decree No. 70/2008/ND-CP mainly regulates the responsibility of various government agencies in the area of gender equality and coordination between these agencies in the management of this area. Decree No. 48/2009/ND-CP sets out detailed regulations on (i) information, education, and communication on gender and gender equality; (ii) inclusion of gender equality issues in draft legal documents; (iii) measures to promote gender equality; and (iv) financial sources for gender equality activities. In addition, for violations of the Law on Gender Equality, the Decree No. 55/2009/ND-CP dated 10 June 2009 on sanctioning of administrative violation of gender equality is also enacted to provide for acts of administrative violation of gender equality, sanctioning forms and levels, and sanctioning competence.

Target beneficiaries. Women

Results indicators/Targets. Level of gender equality-specific actions in the development of subsequent legal documents.

Decision No. 939/QD-TTg

Decision No. 939/QD-TTg was passed on 30 June 2017 as part of a project "Supporting Women Entrepreneurship in the period of 2017–2025" (Project 939).

Objectives. Decision No. 939/QD-TTg aims to raise awareness of women's enterprise development in legal guidelines and policies, promote the realization of business ideas for women-owned enterprises, and contribute to the implementation of national goals on enterprise development and the National Strategy on Gender Equality.

Implementing agencies. Central Viet Nam Women's Union, Ministry of Finance, other relevant ministries and agencies; People's Committees of provinces and municipalities.

Associated decrees and circulars. None.

Target beneficiaries. Includes women who have ideas and want to start a business, cooperative groups or cooperatives, and new businesses established by women. Priority is given to women from poor and disadvantaged households, women from ethnic minorities, women with disabilities, and women living in difficult areas and areas where agricultural land has been converted.

Results indicators/Targets. Support 20,000 women starting businesses, have 100,000 newly established women's businesses provided with consultancy and support for enterprise development.

Not specific to Women in Business

Law on Enterprises, 2020

The Law on Enterprises was passed by the National Assembly in June 2020 replacing an earlier version of the same law from 2014. It has been in effect since 1 January 2021. The law covers the establishment, management, reorganization, dissolution, and relevant activities of enterprises.

Objectives. (i) Creating favorable conditions for the establishment of enterprises in Viet Nam; (ii) providing fair treatment to all investors; (iii) creating an enabling environment and reducing the cost for corporate governance and company restructuring; (iv) providing better protection for legitimate rights and benefits of investors, shareholders, and members of enterprises; (v) creating favorable conditions and reducing costs for the exit of enterprises, investors from the market, and (vi) improving state management efficiency toward enterprises.

Implementing agencies. Ministry of Planning and Investment, Provincial Business Registration Bureau

Associated decrees and circulars. Decree No. 47/2021/ND-CP sets out detailed regulations on state-owned enterprises, social enterprises, groups of companies, defense and security enterprises, and disclosure of information. Decree No. 01/2021/ND-CP which is guided by Circular No. 01/2021/TT-BKHDT dated 16 March 2021 of Ministry of Planning and Investment deals with necessary documents and procedures for registration of enterprises and household businesses, and regulation on business registration authorities and state management on registration of enterprises and household businesses.

Target beneficiaries. Limited liability companies, joint-stock companies, partnerships, sole proprietorships, and groups of companies.

Results indicators/Targets. None.

Law on Investment, 2020

The Law on Investment was passed by the National Assembly on 17 June 2020 to replace an earlier version of the same law from 2014. It has been in effect since 1 January 2021. In general, the law deals with both inward and outward business investment activities, investment incentives, priority and conditional investment sectors, supporting policies, and procedures for establishing and implementing investment projects in Viet Nam from domestic and foreign sources.

Objectives. (i) Improving the quality and efficiency in attracting domestic and foreign investment, in particular, the development of sectors and locations concerning national security and defense, sustainable development, and environment protection; (ii) completing regulations on conditional business activities and business conditions, reducing unreasonable and unnecessary conditional business lines to ensure the rights to engage in business for individuals and enterprises; (iii) creating more favorable conditions for investment activities, cutting costs, and administrative procedures in investment activities; and (iv) completing management mechanisms between central and local government authorities to enhance state management efficiency.

Implementing agencies. Ministry of Planning and Investment, Provincial Business Registration Bureau.

Associated decrees and circulars: Decree No. 29/2021/ND-CP dated 26 March 2021 prescribing procedures for the appraisal of projects of national significance and supervision and assessment of investments. Circular No. 03/TT-BKHDT dated 09 April 2021 offers guiding templates for documents and reports related to investment activities in Viet Nam, outward investment activities, and investment promotion activities. The primary supporting regulation is Decree No. 31/2021/ND-CP, which details business lines and conditions for market access by foreign investors, guarantees for business investment, investment incentives, overseas investment activities, investment promotion, and management.

Target beneficiaries. Investors, agencies, organizations, and individuals involved in business investment activities.

Results indicators/Targets. None.

Resolutions No. 02/NQ-CP

Resolution No. 02/NQ-CP was promulgated on 1 January 2019 as an update to Resolution No. 19/NQ-CP on implementing key tasks and measures toward improving the business environment and increasing national competitiveness. Resolution No. 02/NQ-CP is broader in scope than Resolution No. 19/NQ-CP and focuses on removing barriers to business in all fields.

Objectives. To increase the ranking of Viet Nam on business environment and competitiveness capacity as measured by the World Bank in terms of business environment, World Economic Forum in terms of competitiveness capacity, World Intellectual Property Organization's Global Innovation Index, and the UN in terms of indexes for e-Government development.

Implementing agencies. Ministry of Planning and Investment, Ministry of Finance, Ministry of Science and Technology, Ministry of Natural Resources and Environment, Ministry of Industry and Trade, Vietnam Chamber of Commerce and Industry

Associated decrees and circulars. Resolution No. 19/NQ-CP, Decision No. 749/QD-TTg

Target beneficiaries: SMEs

Results indicators/Targets. None.

Resolution No. 35NQ-CP

Resolution No. 35/NQ-CP was passed in May 2016, as part of the Government of Viet Nam's five-year socioeconomic development plan 2016–2020.

Objective. To promote the emergence of internationally competitive Vietnamese enterprises able to develop sustainably by the end of this period.

Implementing agencies. Ministry of Planning and Investment, Ministry of Finance, Ministry of Science and Technology, Ministry of Natural Resources and Environment, Ministry of Industry and Trade, State Bank of Vietnam, Vietnam Chamber of Commerce and Industry

Associated decrees and circulars. Resolution No. 19/2016/NQ-CP on key tasks and measures to improve the business environment and increase national competitiveness over 2016–2017. Resolution No. 36a/NQ-CP on e-government aims to create opportunities for enterprises to follow work performed by state agencies through the internet. Resolution No. 225/QD-TTg on the approval of the

Plan for Public Administration Reform 2016–2020. Decision No. 09/2015/QD-TTg on implementation of a one-stop-shop and interconnected one-stop-shops at local state administrative agencies.

Target beneficiaries. Privately owned businesses.

Results indicators/Targets. Private sector contributing 48%–49% of annual gross domestic product (GDP).

Resolution 10/NQ-TW and Resolution 98/NQ-CP

Resolution No. 98/NQ-CP was issued by the Government of Viet Nam on 3 October 2017 as the action plan for Resolution No. 10-NQ/TW. It advises all levels and branches of government on how to go about implementing the directives issued under the previous resolution. Resolution No. 10-NQ/TW was issued by The Central Executive Committee of the Communist Party of Viet Nam in July 2017. It relates to improving business and regulatory processes to create a more favorable investment environment for private economic development.

Objectives. (i) Create a mechanism for the private economic sector to develop more effectively, sustainably, and healthily; (ii) motivate private business in a socialist-oriented market economy; (iii) contribute to fast and sustainable socioeconomic development; (iv) constantly improve people's living standards; (v) enhance social progress and social justice; (vi) ensure national defense and security; and (vii) turn Viet Nam into a modern industrialized country.

Implementing agencies. Ministry of Planning and Investment, Ministry of Finance, Ministry of Science and Technology, Ministry of Natural Resources and Environment, Ministry of Industry and Trade

Associated decrees and circulars. None.

Target beneficiaries. Investors, privately owned businesses

Results indicators/Targets. By 2020: 1 million enterprises operating; the private sector contributes 50% of GDP.

Resolution No. 68/NQ-CP

Resolution No. 68/NQ-CP was issued on 12 May 2020 and relates to cutting and simplifying business regulations during 2020–2025.

Objectives. To reduce the regulatory burden required for start-ups and established businesses by cutting and simplifying the number of regulations, reducing costs associated with regulatory compliance, and minimizing the number of documents for business registrations.

Implementing agencies. Led by the Office of Government with implementation responsibility born on all ministries, ministerial agencies, and government agencies.

Associated decrees and circulars. Decree No. 61/2018/ND-CP on implementing a one-stop-shop for administrative procedures and Decree No. 45/2020/ND-CP regulating the provision of online public services on the National Public Service Portal. Resolution No. 50/NQ-CP dated 20/5/2021 separately highlighted the mission of reviewing and abolishing barriers to business rights.

Target beneficiaries. Enterprises, citizens.

Results indicators/Targets. Cut and simplify at least 20% of the number of regulations, and reduce at least 20% of costs of compliance with regulations by 2025.

COVID-19 Supporting Policies

As part of the review of COVID-19 support policies, five policies were examined: Resolution No. 42/NQ-CP (amended by Resolution No. 154/NQ-CP), Resolution No. 84/NQ-CP, Resolution No. 68/NQ-CP (amended by Resolution No. 126/NQ-CP), Resolution No. 105/NQ-CP, and Resolution No. 11/NQ-CP/2022. These resolutions focused on activities such as tax and social insurance reductions, loan support, debt relief, land rent deferrals, and allowances for quarantine and healthcare requirements.

Objectives. To provide support for employees, employers, and people facing difficulties due to the COVID-19 pandemic, contribute to the recovery of production and business, mitigate the negative effects of the pandemic, and stabilize production, business, and guarantee people and employees' life and safety.

Implementing agencies. Ministry of Labor, War Invalids and Social Affairs, Ministry of Finance

Associated decrees and circulars. Decree No. 92/2021/ND-CP issuing solutions to support enterprises and people affected by COVID-19; Decision No. 15/2020/QD-TTg on implementation of policies on assistance for people affected by COVID-19 pandemic; Decree No. 31/2022/ND-CP on interest subsidies provided by state budgets for loans to enterprises, cooperatives, and household businesses; Circular No. 83/2020/TT-BTC guiding Decision No. 15/2020/QD-TTg; Decision No. 23/2021/QD-TTg on implementation of certain policies to support employees; Circular No. 05/2020/TT-NHNN of the State Bank of Vietnam concerning loan refinancing for grants to the Viet Nam Bank for social policies under Decision No. 15/2020/QD-TTg; Circular No. 03/2022/TT-NHNN on instructions for commercial banking implementation of interest rate support by Decree No. 31/2022/ND-CP.

Other supporting policies are provided in Decree No. 41/2020/ND-CP on tax and land rent deferral, Decree No. 52/2021/ND-CP on deferral of value-added tax, corporate income tax, personal income tax, and land rents in 2021, and Decree No. 15/2022/ND-CP on tax exemption and reduction under Resolution No. 43/2022/QH15 of National Assembly on fiscal and monetary policies for supporting socioeconomic recovery and development program.

Target beneficiaries. Existing business owners and employees

Results indicators/Targets. By the end of 2021, at least 1 million enterprises, cooperatives, and business households will receive credit support.

www.ingramcontent.com/pod-product-compliance
Lightning Source LLC
Chambersburg PA
CBHW050043220326
41599CB00045B/7266